BACH'S ORNAMENTS

BACH'S ORNAMENTS

BY

WALTER EMERY

NOVELLO AND CO LTD
160 WARDOUR STREET
LONDON W·I

FIRST PRINTED IN 1953
REPRINTED IN 1954
REPRINTED IN 1957
REPRINTED IN 1961

Set in Monotype Bembo
Printed and bound in Great Britain
by Novello and Company Limited
Hollen Street, London W.1

CONTENTS

6 CONTENTS

PREFACE

THIS book deals with the ornaments that Bach indicated by signs; not with the inaccurate rhythmical notation that was common in the eighteenth century. The chief types of inaccurate notation are familiar (♩. ♬ instead of ♩ ♪♪♪; ♪. ♪ instead of ♪. ♪ or ♪. ♪; and the use of simple-time notation when compound time is intended—¾ ♫ or ♪. ♪ instead of ⁹⁄₈ ♩ ♪); but so little is known of how far the second and third conventions apply to Bach, and personal feelings are so strong at present, that discussion is profitless.

Silences d'articulation—the tiny rests that may be observed before or after certain ornaments—are almost entirely disregarded. They come under the heading of phrasing rather than of ornamentation, and thus are personal matters.

The only early authorities quoted in this book are well-known ones, and most of the Bach examples come from a handful of his keyboard works. There are various reasons for this. The well-known authors are, on the whole, the likeliest to have thought as Bach did. Again, the ornaments in Bach's vocal and instrumental parts are, as a rule, fewer and simpler than those in his keyboard works. Thus, problems that arise in the vocal and instrumental parts can usually be solved, if they are soluble at all, by comparison with the keyboard works; but the converse is not true. Finally, one cannot deduce Bach's habits from ornaments that he did not write. As things stand, this means that unless a writer on ornamentation has made himself competent to edit every work he wishes to quote, he must take examples only from reproductions of autograph manuscripts, and from a few texts whose reliability can easily be tested. The Bach examples in this book have been chosen in this way; with a few exceptions, included for special reasons and expressly described as questionable, they are authentic beyond all reasonable doubt.

The table of References and Abbreviations (p. 154) will serve also as a list of the authors to whom I am chiefly indebted. Five of them require special mention. Dannreuther and Dolmetsch remain invaluable as sources of general information, despite the misprints that disfigure early issues of the latter, and all copies of the former. Professor W. J. Mitchell's translation of Emanuel Bach, though not flawless, enables one to study the complicated workings of Emanuel's mind without buying the rare original or spending hours in libraries. Landshoff's edition of the Inventions, with its accompanying *Revisionsbericht*, is a perfect mine of information. Kreutz, whose work is referred to in the Postscript, holds views that are unconventional by English standards, and correspondingly stimulating.

I am also indebted to Miss Eva J. O'Meara, for permission to reproduce the Explication and the manuscript of Ex. 259: to the Trustees of the British Museum, for all the other reproductions: to various Continental librarians, for microfilms: to Messrs Carl Dolmetsch and Ralph Downes, for Ex. 245: to Mr Downes again, for Ex. 246: to Dr William Cole, who undertook the laborious task of reading the whole book in manuscript: and to Mr Basil Ramsey, Mr Desmond Ratcliffe, and my wife, for assistance in proof-reading.

It is hardly necessary to say that the persons named above are not to be held responsible for my opinions.

W.E.

INTRODUCTION

FOR English readers the standard book on ornamentation is *The Interpretation of the Music of the Seventeenth and Eighteenth Centuries*, by Arnold Dolmetsch. Formerly there was also Edward Dannreuther's *Musical Ornamentation*; but this has long been out of print.

Valuable as they are, there is something rather discouraging about both books. They make one feel that Bach's ornamentation can be reduced to a system, and should present no problems to anyone who has mastered either book. This is probably the last impression that the authors wished to convey; but there is no doubt that they do convey it, if only by casual remarks. For instance, during his discussion of Bach's appoggiaturas Dolmetsch says, 'The rule is clear.' Anyone who reads the next few pages—which give other rules, not to mention exceptions—is likely to conclude that this rule is very far from clear to *him*; and with that he will be tempted to throw up the sponge and begin to omit appoggiaturas wholesale, feeling that it is better to omit them than to interpret them wrongly.

As a matter of fact, it is a mistake to think in terms of rules at all; for very little is known about Bach's own interpretations. His one ornament table—the Explication—is hopelessly inadequate, and the contemporary textbooks are not very helpful. They are not always intelligible; when they are intelligible, they are apt to contradict each other; and no-one knows which of them agrees most closely with Bach's own practice.

Attempts to find out what Bach himself played are doomed to failure, for lack of evidence. They are also, almost certainly, a waste of time. It is unlikely that Bach always played his ornaments in exactly the same way. It is certain that the purchasers of his published works would have played the ornaments in all kinds of different ways;

and Bach made not the slightest attempt to prevent this, for, unlike some of his contemporaries, he did not publish ornament tables. He evidently regarded ornamentation as the business of the individual player.

There is no absolutely right tempo for any piece; there are many right tempi, each valid for a certain performer, on a certain day, in a certain building. Similarly, there are no absolutely right schemes of ornamentation; but many schemes, each valid in certain circumstances. The player should put aside all ideas of absolute rightness, and aim instead at an attainable goal—a consistent personal style of ornamentation that will serve, like his phrasing and tempi, to distinguish his Bach-playing from other people's.

He ought to approach an ornament with mixed feelings— of responsibility towards Bach, and freedom to do what he likes when that responsibility has been discharged. The player is responsible for finding out whether Bach wrote the ornament in question: in practical terms, he ought to play from a good edition. He is also responsible for finding out how the sign in question was interpreted during the first half of the eighteenth century: in practical terms, he ought to study the modern textbooks. Having done these things, however, he is free to choose that interpretation which is best authenticated, or (in really difficult cases) that which strikes him as the most musicianly.

The object of this book is to present a substantial amount of eighteenth-century evidence, with all its confusions and contradictions: to point out ambiguities in Bach's notation: and to discuss a considerable number of doubtful passages. In some of these passages it is impossible to apply the two or three so-called rules that have become common knowledge. Of the resulting problems, a few have been left frankly unsolved; and my solutions, when given, are to be regarded as suggestions. The player must always weigh the historical evidence for himself and apply his own musical judgement, if he is to arrive at interpretations convincing in themselves and consistent with each other.

The process is easier than it sounds. Moreover, it is interesting, calling as it does for constant exercise of the critical and musical faculties. Finally, it gives confidence, and this is essential. It is only when a reasonable degree of confidence has been attained that one can begin to play ornaments habitually, and so gain experience enough to play them well.

SOURCES OF THE QUOTATIONS

J. S. Bach

The sources of the music examples are given in the headings. Most of those taken from the Second Part of the Well-tempered Clavier are based on the British Museum Autograph. In other cases, the word *Autograph* means that the example is based on a photograph, or published facsimile, of a manuscript in Bach's hand. OE means that it is based on an Original Edition, published during his lifetime. In examples taken from the Italian Concerto and French Overture OE has a more comprehensive meaning: all but one of the extant copies of the original edition have been examined, and sundry manuscripts as well.

Examples based on modern editions are marked BG, Peters, Bischoff, etc. When two editions are named, it means that two editors, both working from the original manuscripts, arrived at the same conclusion—or, when one of the editions is bracketed, at conclusions that differ only in unessentials.

Other seventeenth- and eighteenth-century authorities

Except Ex. 24, all quotations, verbal and musical, have been taken direct from the original publications.

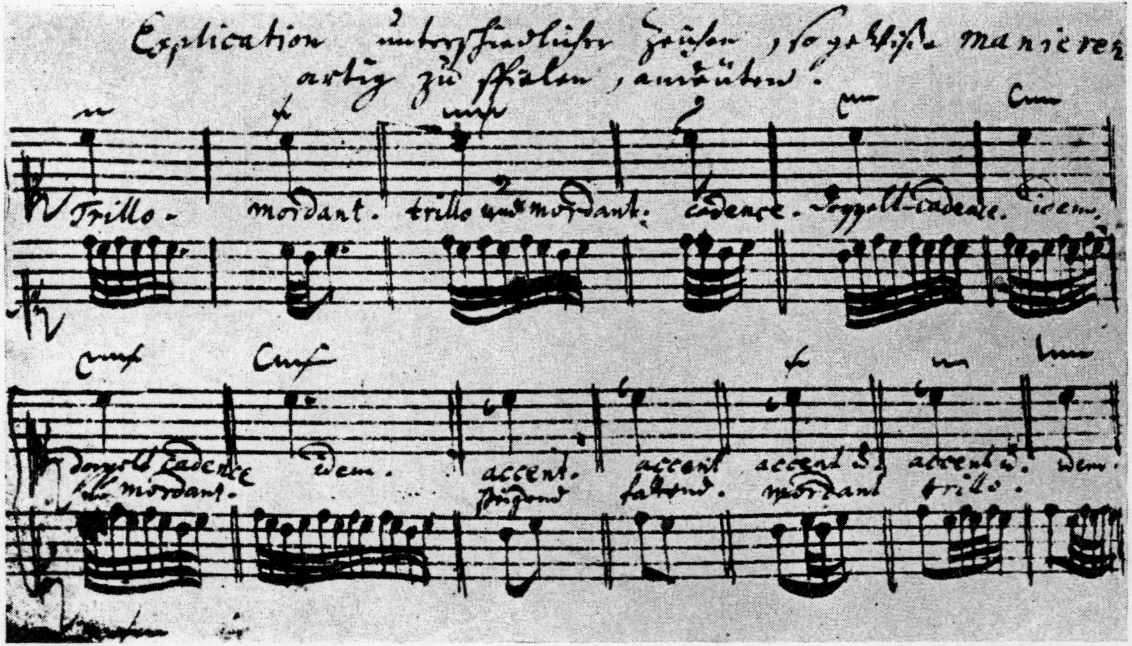

THE EXPLICATION

Explication unterschiedlicher Zeichen, so gewisse *manieren*
artig zu spielen, andeuten.

Explanation of various signs, showing how to play
certain ornaments neatly.

THE Explication is the only ornament table Bach ever drew
up. It occurs at the beginning of the *Clavierbüchlein vor
Wilhelm Friedemann Bach,* and was presumably written in
January 1720. The original manuscript is in the Library of
the School of Music of Yale University.

To avoid undue reduction, the lowest staves on the page
have been omitted from the reproduction. They contain

nothing but a large blot, beneath the ornament in the bottom left-hand corner. The notes underlying the blot cannot be read with certainty; and they, like the ornament, may not have been written by Bach.

Bach's terminology is for the most part obsolete. In the following list it is translated into the terms used in this book, which agree fairly closely with those used by Dannreuther and Dolmetsch.

1. Trillo: a rather short shake (pp. 69, 124).
2. Mordant: mordent (p. 19).
3. Trillo und mordant: long shake with closing-notes (pp. 37, 62).
4. Cadence: turn (p. 31).
5. Doppelt-cadence: long shake with ascending prefix (p. 55).
6. Long shake with descending prefix (p. 55); *not* the same as No. 5.
7. Doppelt-cadence und mordant: long shake with ascending prefix and closing-notes (pp. 55, 62).
8. Long shake with descending prefix and closing-notes (pp. 55, 62); *not* the same as No. 7.
9. Accent steigend: rising appoggiatura (p. 76).
10. Accent fallend: falling appoggiatura (p. 76).
11. Accent und mordant: rising appoggiatura and mordent (p. 22).
12. Accent und trillo: falling appoggiatura and short shake (pp. 76, 124).
13. The same as no. 12.

Bach wrote the Explication with his own hand, and it is authoritative as far as it goes. Unfortunately it does not go very far; its value has, indeed, been greatly exaggerated. It is nothing more than a rough guide, made for a boy of ten who did not need anything better because he was being taught by his father, and largely on his father's music. Like so many other eighteenth-century ornament tables, it treats ornaments without regard to their context; and there are two other things to be borne in mind. Firstly, very few

composers can be trusted to produce, without critical assist-
ance, a clear comprehensive exposition of their own practice.
Secondly, Bach may have changed his mind, as Gottlieb
Muffat did. The latter published his *Componimenti* and
72 *Versetl* within a few years of each other, round about 1730.
Each book has an ornament table, and the two tables differ
(Ex. 1). It cannot be proved that Bach was any more con-

Ex. 1   Gottlieb Muffat

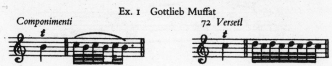

Componimenti   72 *Versetl*

sistent; and it follows that the Explication may not be strictly
applicable either to his early works or to the Goldberg
Variations of 1742.

The signs that occur in actual compositions are not always
as easy to distinguish as those in the Explication. A few
specimens are reproduced on p. 150.

AUXILIARY NOTES

MOST ornaments involve auxiliary or passing-notes. There
is plenty of eighteenth-century evidence that, with rare
exceptions, such notes should be played diatonically—not
necessarily within the key of the piece, but within the key
that is in force at the moment. Thus, the shake in Ex. 2 is
played with ♮*a″*, the key being G minor. On the other hand,

Ex. 2   WK I, Prelude in G minor, bar 1.   BG and Bischoff

the shake in Ex. 3 (which certainly ought to be played,
whether or no Bach wrote it) takes ♭*a″*, because the key is,
at the moment, C minor. See also Ex. 4.

Ex. 3 Organ Toccata in D minor, bars 88–9. BG and Peters

Ex. 4 WK II, Fugue in A minor, bar 21. Autograph

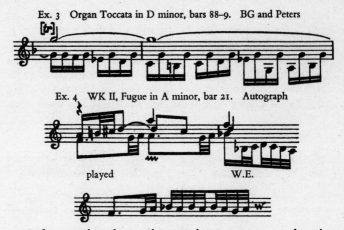

played   W.E.

Unfortunately, players do not always agree on what the key is, as in Ex. 5. The authenticity of these ornaments is very doubtful, but they are undeniably effective; and as they are often played, it is necessary to discuss them.

Ex. 5 'Little' E minor Organ Fugue, bars 1–4. Peters (BG)

played

bar 1   bar 3   W.E.

The mordents in bar 1 were formerly played with $\sharp a$ as the auxiliary note. It is probable that no-one does this nowadays; the key is undoubtedly E minor, and if the auxiliary is to be diatonic, it must be $\natural a$. The treatment of the mordents in bar 3, however, is still in dispute. There are some

who maintain that this bar is in B minor, apparently for no
better reason than that it contains the fugal answer, and
some textbooks say that fugal answers are in the dominant.

Textbooks and examination fugues have very little to do
with Bach's music. His answers do not always touch the
dominant key at all; and when they do, they are just as likely
to modulate half-way through the answer as at its beginning.
There is a sensible discussion of this matter in G. Oldroyd,
The Technique and Spirit of Fugue, pp. 52–98; but the best way
to find out what Bach did is to examine his fugues oneself.

In Ex. 5, it is evident that bars 1 and 2 establish the key of
E minor, and that the key of the piece will remain E minor
until something disturbs it. This something happens in bar 4;
not in bar 3. Bar 3, then, is still in E minor, and the mordents should be played with the leading-note ($\sharp d$). To play
them with $\natural d$ is to force a modulation into B minor a bar
earlier than it is called for by the notes Bach wrote.

Again, there are some who argue that if the mordents in
bar 1 are played with $\natural a$, all the other mordents must be
played with whole-tone auxiliaries (such as $\natural d$ in bar 3), to
secure consistency; but they give the word an unnecessarily
wide meaning. Consistency requires that mordents should
be played at every entry of the subject in this fugue; it does
not require that the auxiliary note should always be a tone
below the main note.

In the rest of this fugue, the auxiliaries should be played
as follows: bars 6–7, $\natural a'$: 10, $\sharp d'$: 12–13, $\natural e$: 19, $\natural a$: 24–5,
$\natural d''$: 27–8, $\natural a'$: 33–4, $\natural A$.

Very occasionally one may come across a passage in which
a diatonic auxiliary seems wrong (Ex. 6). In such cases—at

Ex. 6   Organ Sonata I. ii. 9–10.   Autograph

played　　　　　　　　W.E.

any rate when the ornament is a mordent—one need not
hesitate to sharpen the auxiliary; for within a few years of
Bach's death, at the latest, mordents were commonly played
with auxiliaries a semitone below the main note, whether
chromatic or not.　This was supposed to make the mordents
more brilliant (C.P.E.B., Mordent, §11; Agricola, p. 114).

Modern editions often specify auxiliary notes by small
superimposed accidentals.　The vast majority of these accidentals are editorial, and it is safest to assume that they all
are.　No doubt most of them are right; but there is no need
to observe them with superstitious reverence.

CONSECUTIVES

THE question of Bach's attitude to consecutives must be
touched on here, for although it arises surprisingly seldom,
it is of great importance when it does arise.　This is not
the place for a detailed discussion; indeed, no such discussion
is possible at present.　Passages where consecutives occur—
perhaps simply because Bach forgot to correct them—have
often been noted; but passages where he corrected them have
usually been recorded only when the corrections happen to
be significant in some other way.　Examination of current
editions and their prefaces would therefore give an exaggerated impression of Bach's tolerance.　The truth will only
be discovered by studying actual MSS, preferably of works
that were hastily sketched and heavily corrected.

Emanuel Bach insists (Appoggiatura, §§16, 17: and Trill,
§29) that ornament-interpretations must not give rise to
consecutives, however transient.　No doubt he was more
sensitive to consecutives than his father, or certain other
musicians of his father's generation (Mitchell, p. 203, §3 and

note 5: F. T. Arnold, *Thorough-Bass*, p. 393); but this additional sensitivity seems to have been concerned with what may be called *near*-consecutives, and with evasions in continuo realizations. There is at present nothing to suggest that *real* consecutives in obbligato parts were any less objectionable to Sebastian than to Emanuel. Sebastian would correct them, if he happened to notice them, even when they were well hidden in the middle of a five-part choral texture: those who have access to the facsimile score of the B minor Mass should examine the corrections at bars 61 and 115 of the first chorus.

For the present, therefore, Emanuel Bach's ruling must be accepted; and for that matter, it is not likely that any future discovery will justify the introduction of *real* consecutives, however transient, between extreme parts or in a thin texture.

This matter is referred to in the footnote to p. 42, and in the discussion of Exx. 28, 71, 158, 206, and 290. So far as long shakes are concerned, it will be understood that these remarks apply only to their beginnings, and not to any consecutives that arise during their repercussions. The shake in the G minor Prelude of WK I, at bar 3, will serve as an example.

THE MORDENT

SOME English writers call this ornament the Inverted Mordent or Lower Mordent; but, as the Explication shows, Bach called it simply Mordant.

The sign is ∿, and the interpretation is usually as given in the Explication and Ex. 7. Very occasionally one may feel

Ex. 7 WK II, Fugue in C, bars 1–2. Autograph

W.E.

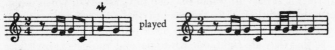

inclined to adopt the interpretation of Ex. 13; rather more

frequently, when the sign applies to a long note, it is effective
to play a Long Mordent. This involves nothing more than
an increase in the number of repercussions (p. 23). In general,
therefore, the mordent is the most straightforward of all
ornaments.

Mordents have sometimes been misread and printed as
shakes, as in the first impression (1735) of the Italian Concerto and French Overture. It is quite possible that mistakes
of the same kind have been made elsewhere, and have not
yet been detected.

On the other hand, a mordent has sometimes displaced a
shake. In Ex. 8, the sign should be ⚹ (a shake with closing-

Ex. 8   Organ Prelude in G, bar 45.   BG

Ex. 9   Gamba Sonata II. i. 13.   BG

notes), as at the end of the movement; in Ex. 9, probably
tr. This type of error may sometimes be due to the fact
that in a cramped manuscript Bach would write a short
shake (⚹) across the stem of its note.* Schicht, who edited
the Canonic Variations about 1804, was misled in this way;
and it may be that later editors have sometimes fallen into
the same trap.

It is necessary to watch for such mistakes, even when using
the best editions. As the manuscripts and original editions
can seldom be consulted, and there is in any case no guaran-
tee that they are right, one has to depend on one's knowledge

* See the reproduction, p. 150, no. 7.

of Bach's habits. In the cadential contexts of Exx. 8–9 a mordent is always wrong; the ornament must be a shake or a turn
(Exx. 37, 242).   In other contexts, a mordent is generally
right in ascending passages, just as a short shake (⁕) is in
descending passages.   The quickest way of grasping the
difference is to learn the movement from which Ex. 10 is
taken.

Ex. 10   French Overture, Gigue, bars 3–7.   OE

Nevertheless, there is no clear rule. The mordent in Ex. 11
is not at all what one would expect, but it is in Bach's own
copy of the original edition; similarly with the second and
third mordents in Ex. 12, which is autograph.

Ex. 11   French Overture, Passepied II, bars 18–19.   OE

Ex. 12   XVIII, no. 14, *Allein Gott*, bars 1–2.   Autograph

A mordent was sometimes played by striking both notes
together and immediately releasing the lower one, somewhat
as in Ex. 13. This technique, according to Emanuel Bach,
was employed only on detached notes (cf. Ex. 229).

Ex. 13   W.E.

A mordent is sometimes slurred to the previous note, as
in Ex. 14.* The slur can then be treated as a tie. It appears that

* In the edition of 1742 this ornament looks like a Long Mordent; but the
original editions cannot be trusted in such details as this. In Anna Magdalena
Bach's manuscript of this Aria (Berlin MS P 225) the mordent is an ordinary
short one. Those who prefer a Long Mordent need not hesitate to play it.

there is no direct eighteenth-century evidence for this inter-

Ex. 14   Goldberg Variations, Aria, bar 1.   OE

pretation; but it is effective, and the indirect evidence is
strong. If a slur is to be treated as a tie when combined with
a shake or turn in a descending context (Exx. 42, 86, 261),
there seems no reason why it should not be treated similarly
when combined with a mordent in an ascending context—
so long as there is movement in another part.

A mordent may be preceded by a rising appoggiatura
(Ex. 15). The interpretation given is in accordance with the

Ex. 15   Orgelbüchlein, *Wenn wir*, bars 8–9.   Autograph

played   W.E.

Explication; but a tied interpretation (an 'Inverted Pralltriller') is justified by Ex. 16, and is often effective—again,
so long as there is movement in another part. In Ex. 15
there is no such movement.

Ex. 16   Agricola, p. 103, note 1

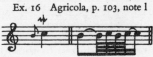

As in Ex. 10, mordents often serve as accents; and for this
reason they are generally played fast. On a long note in a
slow expressive piece, and in such passages as Exx. 14 and
15, a mordent can be taken more gently; but the speed

cannot be slackened very much without destroying the point of the ornament. If a slight slackening is not enough, the ordinary mordent should be replaced by a long one.

THE LONG MORDENT

THE sign used in modern editions is ⋀⋁ or ⵖⵖ, with the vertical stroke centred or on the left; not on the right, as in the sign for a shake with closing-notes (⋀⋁).

This sign is not in the Explication, and I do not remember having seen an unmistakable example of it in a Bach autograph. In the original editions there are signs that can be taken for long mordents (Ex. 17); but these editions are not

Ex. 17 Organ Fugue in E flat, end. OE

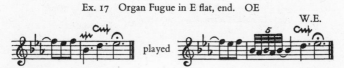

altogether reliable. It is quite possible that Bach never deliberately wrote anything but the ordinary short sign (⋀⋁); he would probably have said it was the player's business to deduce the length of the mordent from the length of the note. This seems to have been Muffat's opinion (Ex. 18), and was certainly Couperin's. The latter wrote, 'It is the value of the notes that must determine the lengths of mordents, *ports-de-voix*, and shakes—the word *length* meaning the number of repercussions' (1713, p. 74).

Ex. 18 Gottlieb Muffat, 72 Versetl, *c*. 1730

The position is that when a Long Mordent appears in a reputable modern edition, it is probably right. The editor may have misinterpreted the manuscript or original edition from which he was working; but he is not likely to have printed an unusual ornament without satisfying himself that it is appropriate. Further, the long mordent can, as suggested above, be substituted for the ordinary one when the latter is unsatisfactory—that is, on long notes. It might, for instance, be used in Ex. 19 as well as in Ex. 17; and in some

Ex. 19   Italian Concerto. ii. 4.   OE

might be played   W.E.

cases the number of repercussions might be still further increased.

Some authors say that a mordent, whether short or long, must never occupy the whole length of the note (C.P.E.B., Mordent, §8, and Türk, p. 277). In Bach, exceptions to this rule seem to be rare; but one has recently been discovered, and others may follow. See p. 146.

THE SLIDE

THE Slide is indicated by ⟿ or by two small notes. As Bach did not include either sign in the Explication, their meaning has to be deduced from contemporary sources.

The sign ⟿ was used by Kuhnau. Unfortunately he did not explain it in musical notation; in his preface of 1689 he simply referred to Ex. 20, and gave an obscure verbal

Ex. 20   J. Kuhnau, Neuer Clavier Ubung I, p. 11 (1689)

description.* Comparison with Heinichen (Ex. 285) suggests that the slurred passages in Ex. 20 are written-out slides.
A similar interpretation might serve in Ex. 21, bar 1; but
could hardly be applied to Ex. 21, bar 2, to the sign in the

Ex. 21   J. Kuhnau, Neuer Clavier Übung II, p. 59 (1696)

right-hand part of Ex. 20, bar 5, or to a number of other
passages in Kuhnau's music. It would perhaps be more
satisfactory to treat Ex. 21, bar 1, in one of the ways shown
in Exx. 22–3, and let bar 2 correspond.†

* . . . die Schleüffer . . . , welche besage des Characteris aus der Tertia
entweder drunter oder drüber in die nachgesätzte Note nach dem Exempel
des 4.5. und 6ten Tactes N6 trainiret werden.
. . . the Slide, which runs to the following note from the third below or
above, according to the sign, as in bars 4, 5, and 6 of N6. [These are the
bars quoted in Ex. 20.]

† The sign // is a mordent; the sign / is an Accentus. Of this also Kuhnau
gave only an obscure description; he seems to have meant a kind of appoggiatura, possibly resembling Heinichen's interpretation in Ex. 285.

Ex. 22   W.E.   Ex. 23   W.E.

J. G. Walther gives the sign ᴧᴧ, with an interpretation, in his *Kompositionslehre* of 1708. I have not seen this MS, and have taken Ex. 24 from Hermann Gehrmann's article in *Vierteljahrsschrift für Musikwissenschaft*, Jahrg. 7, p. 521 (Leipzig, 1891).

Ex. 24   J. G. Walther (from Gehrmann)

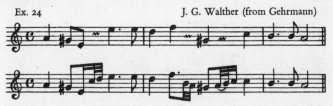

D'Anglebert (1689), Murschhauser (*c.* 1703), Gottlieb Muffat (*c.* 1730), and Marpurg (1755) all used slide-like ornaments, with various names and signs. All their interpretations begin *on* the beat, as in Ex. 23.

Ex. 25 is taken from Emanuel Bach. He regards the small-note sign as the usual one, and remarks that the ornament is always played quickly.

Ex. 25   C.P.E.B., Slide, §§3-4

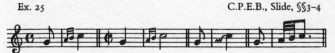

Bach is supposed to have studied Kuhnau in his early years, and perhaps it was from him that he picked up the sign ᴧᶜ. In the 1850's this sign was so unfamiliar that Rietz actually thought it might be peculiar to Bach (BG IV. xxvii); he naturally replaced it by small notes (Ex. 27), and other editors followed his example. Genuine examples of the small-note sign are therefore rarer than modern editions would lead one to suppose; I do not remember having seen one in any of the autographs and first editions that I have had occasion to examine.

From the above discussion it seems to follow that two interpretations of the Slide were current in Bach's day. Walther, and possibly Kuhnau, played it *before* the beat; all the other authorities, *on* the beat. Even if there were any reason to suppose that Walther stood alone, it would be unsafe to disregard his interpretation; for he was intimate with Bach for nine years.

In dealing with a Slide, it is nevertheless wise to begin by playing it *on* the beat, as in Exx. 26–7.* This usually proves satisfactory.

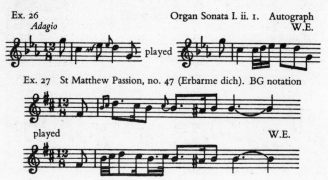

Ex. 26   Organ Sonata I. ii. 1.   Autograph
Adagio   W.E.

played

Ex. 27   St Matthew Passion, no. 47 (Erbarme dich). BG notation

played   W.E.

Sometimes, as in Ex. 28, no other interpretation is possible; if these slides were played before the beat, they would make octaves with the bass. (See also p. 144.)

Ex. 28   Organ Fugue in C. BG
bar 18   bar 43

In a few cases—but only a few—an interpretation of the Walther type may seem more graceful (Exx. 29, 30). See also Exx. 202–3.

* For the interpretation of the small note in Ex. 27, see p. 97.

Ex. 29 XVIII, no. 12, *Allein Gott*, beginning. Autograph

on the beat   played   before the beat   W.E.
                     W.E.

Ex. 30 French Overture, Gavotte II.   OE

bar 2   bar 6   bar 17

In the movement from which Ex. 30 is taken there is a
curious textual problem, whose solution may lie in an interpretation of this type. Ex. 30 is quoted from the original
edition, in which the French Overture as a whole is in B
minor, and this Gavotte is in D; but formerly there was a
version in C minor and E flat, which has been preserved in
a copy made by Anna Magdalena Bach. Her manuscript
contains Ex. 31. The orthodox interpretation, with the slide

Ex. 31   French Overture, Gavotte II, bar 19.   A. M. Bach's MS (P 226)
W.E.

orthodox
interpretation:

on the beat, is manifestly weak; and David, in his edition, rejected it altogether. Regarding the slide as 'probably a mistake', he replaced it by a mordent (Ex. 32).

Ex. 32   David's emendation

As Ex. 32 does not look in the least like Ex. 31, and the resemblance would have been no closer in Bach's writing, it is difficult to see how Anna could have made such a mistake; and David's emendation must be considered unacceptable. It is much simpler to suppose that the slide was meant to be played *before* the beat (Ex. 33).

Ex. 33   Waltherian interpretation

It must be added that in Anna's MS the slide is clearly placed on f'—a fourth, not a third, below the main note. It is not impossible that she meant exactly what she wrote (Ex. 34); but, although D'Anglebert used ornaments of this

Ex. 34   unorthodox interpretation

type, I do not remember any other passage in which a slide of a fourth is likely to be authentic. See, however, the variant in Peters Organ Works VI. 96 (BG XL. 208), bar 10, etc.

It must also be added that in the original edition of this Gavotte there is no ornament of any kind at this point.

Bach sometimes wrote slides out in full, as in Ex. 35. At the beginning of the movement, the slide can be played as written; in bar 73, and again in bar 77, it should be played in triplets.

Ex. 35 Organ Sonata III. iii. Autograph

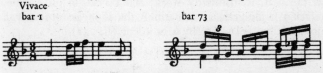

The subject quoted in Ex. 36 contains two slides—the first written out, the second indicated by the usual sign (♪). This

Ex. 36 Gamba Sonata II, Andante. BG

notation is used at every entry of the subject except one. One would normally interpret the ♪ in exactly the same way (rhythmically) as the written-out slide; but the almost consistent use of different notation arouses a faint suspicion that the interpretation ought to be different—faster, perhaps, or *before* the beat.

As Bach wrote it, the sign ♪ sometimes looked like a small quaver.* The slide in bar 17 of Ex. 30 was engraved as an appoggiatura ♯g′ in the second impression of the original edition; and a similar mistake (corrected in the preface) will be found in BG IX, p. 15, bar 7. It is possible that this mistake has been made elsewhere, and that some of the rising appoggiaturas in current editions ought to be replaced by slides.

For some slide-like ornaments indicated by other signs, see Exx. 223–8 and 256–9.

* The reproduction on p. 150, no. 12, will give some idea of how this might happen.

THE TURN

BACH used a sloping sign (see the Explication). It is usually represented by the ordinary horizontal sign (∾); but sometimes, as in Dolmetsch (p. 230), by a vertical one (ⱬ). The meaning is the same. There is no question of confusion with the Inverted Turn ( ), for Bach did not use the latter ornament. Signs that look like Inverted Turns (↭) occur in at least one non-autograph manuscript (Berlin P 218); but they stand for mordents.

In Bischoff's edition of the Three-part Invention in G minor, bar 5, there is a more or less unplayable turn. According to Landshoff, this sign comes from a manuscript known as the pseudo-autograph, and is in fact the letter s, meaning *sinistra*.

When placed over or under a note, a turn is played as in Exx. 37-8, varying according to the tempo.

Ex. 37   WK II, Prelude in E minor, bars 47-8.   Autograph

Ex. 38   The same, bar 59.   Autograph

D'Anglebert gives the interpretation quoted in Ex. 39.

Ex. 39   D'Anglebert

Here the turn is delayed—its first note (c'') would normally
be struck with the d''. This may apply in Ex. 40.

Ex. 40   Three-part Invention in E flat, bar 6.   Autograph of 1723

In legato passages, the first note of a turn can sometimes
be tied (Ex. 41); an interpretation that is to some extent
justified by the slurred turn in Ex. 42.

Ex. 41   XVIII, no. 12, *Allein Gott*, bar 2.   Autograph

Ex. 42   Marpurg, 1755 (Tab. VI, no. 9)

When the turn is placed *between* two notes, the rhythmical details of the interpretation must be settled by the player.

Ex. 43 gives the cadential bars of the two *Grave* sections of the movement. As their functions are similar, it is natural

Ex. 43   French Overture, Ouverture.   OE

to suppose that Bach meant their figuration to be similar, and therefore that bar 162 should be played as in Ex. 44.

Ex. 44   The same, bar 162
                                          W.E.

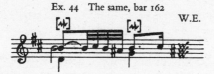

A different pattern is suggested by Ex. 45, taken from two autographs of the same work.

Ex. 45   Two-part Invention in F minor, bar 16

Autograph of 1723   Autograph of 1720

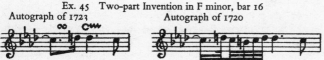

In all such cases the player should bear in mind the evidence of parallel passages (Ex. 43), alternative readings (Ex. 45), and the immediate context as well. In Ex. 46, it seems advisable that the *a″* should be given its full value; Ex. 47, therefore, is probably better than Ex. 48. Compare Ex. 48 with Ex. 45, where there is no skip.

Ex. 46   English Suite in F, Prelude, bar 12.   Peters Urtext and Bischoff

Ex. 47   W.E.   Ex. 48   W.E.

According to Emanuel Bach (Turn, §§2, 10), turns are usually played fast, but can sometimes be broadened out in slow movements (§20).   He gives Ex. 49 as a specimen interpretation, and Ex. 50 as an alternative notation (cf. Ex. 142).   Ex. 51 shows—what Emanuel does not give—the usual notation for Ex. 49.

Ex. 49   C.P.E.B.   Ex. 50   C.P.E.B.   Ex. 51 W.E.

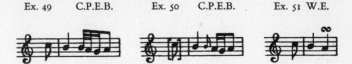

THE SHAKE

BACH indicated 'plain' shakes—those without prefixes or closing-notes—by the letters *t* and *tr*, variously distorted, and by hastily-written wavy lines that are represented in modern editions by the signs ⋀ ⋀⋀. He is said to have used a cross as well (+).

For shakes with specified prefixes and closing-notes he used the signs ⋲⋀ ⋲⋀⋲⋀ ⋲⋀ ⋀ ⊢⋀, and possibly ⋀⋀⊃ and ⋀⋀⊃

The preliminary hook specifies an ascending or descending prefix.

The preliminary vertical stroke specifies an appoggiatura.

The vertical stroke at the end of the sign specifies closing-notes. Note that the stroke comes at the *end* of the sign; not in the middle or at the beginning, as with the Long Mordent (⋀⊢ ⊢⋀).

The final hook (ᵚᵚᴑ ᵚᵚᴑ) may often be an accidental
flourish of the pen; but it is sometimes possible, or even
likely, that Bach used it deliberately to specify closing-notes.
See Exx. 116, 119. Signs of this kind were used by D'Anglebert (1689) and Türk (1789), in both cases meaning closing-
notes (Ex. 52).

Tremblement et pincé

Strange signs sometimes appear in modern editions (e.g.,
ᴄᵚ ᵚᵚᵕ). Some are wrong, others may be conscientious
reproductions of the careless scrawls in the original manuscripts; in any case, they have no special significance. They
can be and should be replaced by one of the regular signs
listed above; the player must ask himself whether the context is suitable for a prefix or closing-notes.

Repercussions

Complicated shakes—those with both prefixes and closing-
notes—cannot be properly formed unless at least eight or
twelve notes are played; for details see p. 56. Otherwise,
there is no rule for the number of repercussions to be used
in shakes; it depends largely on the tempo, and can only be
settled by the player. The eighteenth-century authors are
vague and contradictory; the following suggestions are
sensible, but there is no need to apply any of them to Bach.

A shake can be played slower in a sad piece than in a
cheerful one (Quantz, p. 84, §2).

A shake on a low note can be played slower than one
on a high note (Quantz, p. 85, §6).

A shake can be played at an even speed (Quantz,
p. 84, §5), or at a gradually increasing speed (Couperin,
1717, p. 23).

A shake can be played slower in a large hall than in a small one (Quantz, p. 83, §2).

With these qualifications, Quantz suggests (p. 84, §6) that eight notes should be played to one beat of the pulse. As he reckoned eighty pulse-beats to the minute (p. 267, §55), this means that at ♩=80, shakes should be played in demisemiquavers. Quantz was thinking in terms of the flute of 1752.

It must be clearly understood that the interpretations in this book are not meant to show exactly how many notes should be played.

Plain Shakes: Long or Short?

As will be seen, the answer to this question depends much less on the sign than on the context, and on how many notes can be played at a reasonable tempo. On the one hand, the signs ⁓⁓⁓ *tr* do not necessarily imply long shakes; on the other, the sign ⁓ does not necessarily imply a short shake of three or four notes.

One reason for this ambiguity is that when Bach used the wavy-line sign, he did not count the number of humps in it. The clear distinction between no. 1 and all the other shakes in the Explication is exceptional.* Not being able to reproduce Bach's signs, modern editors have to make do with the two conventional ones (⁓ ⁓⁓⁓); these mean only that in the manuscript sources (which are by no means always autograph) there are wavy lines of some sort.

Further, so far as the length of the shake is concerned, there is no clear distinction between the wavy-line signs and the various forms of *t*. In the manuscript of the Italian Concerto that was sent to the publisher, Bach seems to have indicated a number of shakes by lines in which the wave was almost imperceptible. Some of these shakes are long; others must be short, because they cannot be played in any other way. In the first impression of the original edition most of these

---

* See the reproduction, p. 159, no. 8.

signs were engraved as straight lines. In the second impression they were replaced by the usual signs (~ ~~ c~~). In correcting a copy of the first impression for his own use, Bach was less scrupulous; he obliterated the straight lines as much as possible by the sign *~~*, making no distinction between short and long shakes.*

When it is possible to play more than three or four notes, a long shake may be required, even if the sign is ~. If the note lasts a fairly long time—a minim in a quick tempo, or a quaver in a slow one—a long shake is, on the whole, likely to be right. It is even more likely to be right—whatever the length of the note—if the sign is followed by written-out closing-notes, as in Ex. 96. It would nevertheless be rash to assume that pairs of short notes following shake-signs are always closing-notes; see Ex. 140 and the remarks on it.

The closing-notes of Ex. 96 are of the conventional type. According to Emanuel Bach, other types of figuration can take the place of closing-notes (Ex. 53). Presumably, therefore, these types of figuration also call for long shakes. See Exx. 120–1, 129–31.

Ex. 53   C.P.E.B., Trill, §§13–17

The beginnings of long plain shakes

A long 'plain' shake is indicated by the signs *t*, *tr*, ~~, and very often ~; Ex. 54 gives a strictly orthodox interpretation.

* See the reproductions, p. 150, nos 3-6.

Ex. 54   W.E.

Quantz and Couperin seem often to have prolonged the first note a little, as if it were an appoggiatura (Ex. 55).

Ex. 55   W.E.

There is no reason to suppose that interpretations of this kind ought to be used regularly in Sebastian Bach's music. He had two signs for appoggiatura openings (Explication, nos 12, 13); and as both signs are easy to write, it is reasonable to suppose that when he wanted an appoggiatura opening, he specified it.

On the other hand, eighteenth-century copyists seem sometimes to have replaced Bach's complex shake-signs (～, ～, etc., specifying appoggiaturas and prefixes) by the 'plain' *tr*. Thus it may be that, in works of which there is no extant autograph, some of the *tr*'s ought to be played with appoggiatura openings or prefixes.

In slow movements an appoggiatura opening is sometimes effective, even when it is certain that Bach did not write it; and it is reasonable that players should allow themselves an occasional liberty of this kind.

Setting aside these abnormal interpretations, for which the player must accept full responsibility, it can safely be said that the vast majority of Bach's 'plain' shakes begin as in Ex. 54—on the auxiliary. This statement is supported not only by the Explication, but also by almost all the other ornament tables of the period, whether drawn up by composers whom Bach studied, or by his pupils, or by people who may not have been connected with him in any way.

Unfortunately for present-day players, this agreement was not quite universal. There was an old Italian habit of beginning shakes on the main note (Dannreuther, I. 119; Landow-ska, Bach-Jahrbuch 1910, p. 41).   This habit lasted until Frescobaldi's time (Ex. 56); and Frescobaldi was a composer

Ex. 56   G. Frescobaldi, Toccata II (3rd edn., 1637), end

in whom Bach was interested—he acquired a copy of *Fiori Musicali* in 1714.   As it happens, there are no shakes in *Fiori*; but Bach may have known other works of Frescobaldi's.   In any case, the habit of beginning shakes on the main note was not confined to Italy and to a date fifty years before Bach was born; it extended to Germany during and immediately after Bach's lifetime.   Such interpretations may have been unusual; but it does not follow that Bach never adopted them.

F. X. A. Murschhauser indicated short shakes by the sign *t* both in his *Octi-Tonium* of 1696 and in his *Prototypon* of 1703–7.   He explained the sign only in the latter publication (Ex. 57).   Exx. 58–9 show how it occurs in his music.   The sign resembling a 7 in Ex. 59 is a short appoggiatura.

Ex. 57   Prototypon

Ex. 58   Octitonium, Praeambulum Septimi Toni, bars 3–4

Ex. 59   Prototypon, Fuga [tertia] 12mi Toni

Like Frescobaldi, Murschhauser wrote his long shakes out
in full; many are abnormal, and some begin on the main
note. Ex. 60 shows shakes of two kinds: the right-hand one
beginning on the main note (which is not prolonged), the
left-hand one beginning with a prolonged auxiliary.

Ex. 60   Prototypon, Praeambulum 7timi Toni

Three years after Bach's death, his son Emanuel wrote
(Trill, §5): 'As [the ordinary shake] always begins on the
note above the main note, there is no need to indicate it by
a previous small note (Ex. 61), unless the small note is to be
held as an appoggiatura.'

Ex. 61   C.P.E.B., Trill, §5

As so often happens with ancient textbooks, the full
meaning of this passage is not immediately apparent. It
implies, firstly, that some composers did use small notes to
show that their shakes began with the auxiliary (modern
composers use the sign $\int$ for the same purpose); and,

secondly, that in 1753 a fair number of players began their shakes on the main note—for otherwise there would have been no need for composers to use the precautionary small note. (Compare Exx. 97 and 271–2.)

Anomalous shake-interpretations, then, were undoubtedly in use during the Bach period; but it remains true that most ornament tables show shakes beginning on the auxiliary. Unfortunately, it is also true that in most of the tables the context is disregarded, and the interpretations are mere types. It is by no means certain that the various composers, in playing their own music, always adopted the interpretations given in their ornament tables.

Exx. 62–3, for instance, are taken from Gottlieb Muffat's *Componimenti* of *c.* 1730; and the implied interpretations are shown in Ex. 64. They require a tempo that would be too

Ex. 62 from the ornament table   Ex. 63   from a Gigue, p. 27

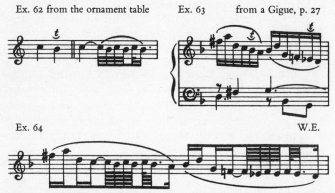

Ex. 64   W.E.

slow for a Gigue; and even if one reduced the number of repercussions, there would still remain a rhythmical hitch due to the tied interpretation of the first shake.

Bach's *Explication* includes five appoggiaturas (nos 9–13); and in each case the appoggiatura takes half the length of the main note. At first sight this looks like a well-established rule; but it takes only very little experience of Bach's music to show that it is nothing of the sort, and one's confidence is not increased by the fact that in nos 12 and 13 the note-

values do not even add up to the correct total. Thus in
nos 1 and 3—a short shake, and a long shake with a 'plain'
beginning—the fact that ~~both~~ interpretations begin on the
auxiliary does not necessarily mean that all Bach's 'plain'
shakes begin in this way without exception.

The shake in Ex. 65 certainly does not. It can be played in

Ex. 65   Organ Fugue in D minor (Dorian), bars 177–184
Pedal   from Berlin MS P 290

quavers, as in the pattern-bar (178); alternatively, it can
break into semiquavers at the *tr*; but in neither case can it
begin on the auxiliary. There is no autograph of this work;
but the copies agree pretty closely in essentials, and the
shake must be accepted as authentic.*

One has therefore to face the fact that although most of
Bach's 'plain' shakes begin on the auxiliary, there are exceptions to this rule; and the question is, when do these exceptions arise?

Dannreuther gave a list of contexts in which he thought
shakes should begin with the main note, and justified most
of them by the assertion that 'melodic or harmonic outlines
should not be blurred' (I. 166). It has long been evident that
he went too far; but it is necessary to discuss his suggestions,
because many players still act on them.

The assertion that 'melodic or harmonic outlines should
not be blurred' is misleading. It would probably be nearer
the truth to say that they were *meant* to be blurred. So far as
Bach's music is written in ordinary notation (large notes),
a good deal of it is not much more than an outline—pur-
posely written as such, so that players should find it easy to
grasp (cf. Exx. 132–3), but not to be taken literally.

In the eighteenth century a shake generally began on the
auxiliary, and thus came to be thought of as a kind of repeated

---

* In the St John Passion, no. 11, bars 22–3, there are other shakes that must
begin on the main note. If begun on the auxiliary, they make octaves. See
also Gamba Sonata I, Finale, bars 37–8.

appoggiatura. An appoggiatura will often smooth over a melodic angularity, or add a touch of harmonic interest to an otherwise undistinguished progression. To interpret a shake in such a way that the 'outline' is preserved in all its melodic angularity and harmonic dullness is (as a rule) almost as bad as to omit the shake altogether.

This must be borne in mind while one considers the contexts in which Dannreuther thought shakes should begin with the main note. They are as follows:*

1. 'When the shake starts *ex abrupto*' [Ex. 66. See also Ex. 2].

Ex. 66   WK II, Fugue in F sharp, beginning.   Autograph

(Repercussions *ad libitum*)   Dannreuther

The shake is on the first note of the subject; and owing to variations of context at some of its later entries, its interpretation is highly disputable.

In bar 32 (Ex. 67) the shake must begin on the auxiliary; and the same is true of bar 64. In all the other entries where

Ex. 67   The same, bar 32

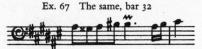

the shake is written as an ornament, the eighteenth-century evidence favours beginning with the auxiliary, and there is no decisive musical evidence against it. Unfortunately, in two places (bars 20 and 70) Bach chose to begin the subject with a sort of slow shake written out in full (Ex. 68); and in both cases the 'slow shake' begins on the main note. The possibility that the figuration of these two bars is to be regarded as a pattern needs no pointing out.

* Mistakes in Dannreuther's examples have been corrected according to the authorities quoted.

Ex. 68 The same

bar 20

bar 70

So far as keyboard technique is concerned, it would have been quite easy to play ordinary shakes in both these bars; Bach must therefore have had some other reason for adopting this variation. If that reason were known, it might provide the clue to the interpretation of all the shakes in this fugue; but for the present one can only say that, except in bars 32 and 64, it is for the player to decide whether he will begin with the main note or with the auxiliary.

Tovey recommended the main note, except in bars 32 and 64; 'otherwise the effect of the beginning abruptly on the leading-note will be spoiled.'

Landowska (Bach-Jahrbuch 1910, pp. 41–2) refused to accept any of Dannreuther's exceptions to the auxiliary-note rule; and in dealing with this one she quoted Couperin (1717, p. 23): 'A shake must always begin with the note a tone or semitone higher than the note it is written on.' The statement looks clear and comprehensive; but it is not valid even for Couperin's music—let alone for Bach's—for two paragraphs later Couperin wrote, 'As for other shakes, they are arbitrary.' His description of these arbitrary shakes is vague in the extreme; but it seems possible that some of them began on the main note. He does not explain how one distinguishes between arbitrary shakes and those that 'always' begin on the auxiliary.

Landowska quotes two Couperin pieces that begin with shakes; but as one cannot be sure that the shakes are not arbitrary, these examples are not very convincing. Her third example is more to the point, in a certain sense, since the initial ornament is an appoggiatura, and there is no doubt about its interpretation. As Couperin was prepared to begin a piece with a chord containing an appoggiatura, he can hardly have had any objection to beginning with a chord containing the initial auxiliary of a normal shake.

Even so, there remains the question of how far Bach was influenced by Couperin. Many players will probably feel that, in contexts of this type, the musical judgement of Tovey and Dannreuther is more trustworthy than arguments based on the confused statements and uncertain practice of composers like Couperin, whose ideas may have differed from Bach's.

2. 'When the shake starts after a note staccato—or after a rest [Ex. 69]. · This case, like that in [Ex. 84], comes under the rule "melodic outlines must not be blurred"—as they would be if the shake were started with the accessory.'

Ex. 69   WK I, Fugue in D minor.   BG and Bischoff

Dannreuther

There is nothing to suggest that Dannreuther was not considering Ex. 69 in isolation; and on that assumption it is very difficult to see why he objected to an orthodox inter-pretation like Ex. 70. Perhaps he subconsciously regarded

Ex. 70 Dolmetsch

this type of context as an extension of the *ex abrupto* type. At all events, the fact that a shake is preceded by a staccato note does not, in itself, justify beginning on the main note.

There may be other facts to be taken into consideration, as indeed there are in this case. Dolmetsch says of Ex. 70, 'It should . . . be reproduced exactly wherever the subject occurs. It is the right way and also the most beautiful' (p. 169). This interpretation makes consecutive fifths in bar 12 (Ex. 71).

Ex. 71 The same
bar 12   According to Dolmetsch

In this fugue it is for the player to decide whether he will follow Dannreuther throughout, or Dolmetsch throughout, or Dolmetsch everywhere except in bar 12. Much depends on the length of the staccato note.

In his heading Dannreuther speaks of shakes that follow a rest; but he does not give an example. This type of context is rather unusual (Ex. 72). It is comparable with the *ex*

Ex. 72   Partita VI, Gigue.   OE

bar 1

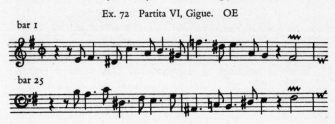

bar 25

abrupto type, and some players will no doubt be inclined to begin both the shakes in Ex. 72 on the main note, instead of adopting the strictly orthodox interpretations of Ex. 73.

Ex. 73

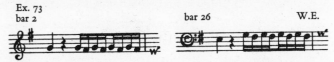

Ex. 72 shows the ornaments as they were engraved. It is a curious fact, and one that may prove to be highly significant, that an early owner of one of the copies of the original edition altered most of the shakes in the second half of this movement to ᴄᴡ. This alteration makes the inversion more exact (Ex. 74). The intelligent eighteenth-century

Ex. 74

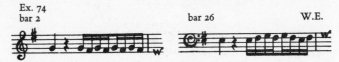

person who made it★ evidently assumed that the shakes in the first half of the movement begin on the auxiliary; and it may safely be said that there is no justification for beginning any of the shakes in this movement on the main note.

3. 'When the repetition of a note is thematic' [Ex. 75; also bars 7 and 19 of the same movement].

Ex. 75   WK I, Prelude in F sharp, bars 12-13.   BG and Bischoff

It is the two starred shakes that Dannreuther is referring to. The imitation is just as strict, and just as intelligible, if one begins with the auxiliary.

★ Possibly Bach. See *Musical Times*, November, 1952.

4. 'When the melody skips, and the shake thus forms part
of some characteristic interval; as, for instance, the interval
of the seventh in [Ex. 76].'

Ex. 76   WK I, Fugue in G, bars 25–6.   BG and Bischoff

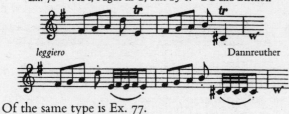

Of the same type is Ex. 77.

Ex. 77   Organ Fugue in F minor, bars 1–2.   BG and Peters

In such cases it is not necessary to preserve the 'characteristic interval'; Bach can be found smoothing such intervals
out, either by using a shake with prefix (Ex. 78) or by in-
serting an appoggiatura (Exx. 178–9). There is no reason
why twentieth-century players should be more scrupulous
about intervals than Bach was; and it follows that in contexts of this type, shakes begin on the auxiliary (Exx. 79, 80).

Ex. 78   WK I, Prelude in F, bars 2–4.   BG and Bischoff

Ex. 79

Ex. 80

5. 'When the movement of the bass would be weakened if the shake were begun with the accessory. This case again comes under the rule: "melodic or harmonic outlines should not be blurred" [Ex. 81].'

Ex. 81   WK II, Fugue in C sharp minor, bar 32.   BG and Bischoff

Exx. 82–3 may perhaps be thought to come under this heading.

Ex. 82   WK II, Fugue in C, bar 8.   Autograph

Ex. 83   WK II, Fugue in G sharp minor, bars 59–60.   Autograph

Dannreuther's statement that an orthodox interpretation
weakens the movement of the bass is a personal opinion.
Some players may agree with him—perhaps neither in his
own example nor in the other two quoted, but in others of
the same type—; but they must remember that there appears
to be no eighteenth-century authority for beginning such
shakes on the main note.

6. Among contexts where the melodic outline is in danger
of being blurred Dannreuther includes those 'where the
preceding note is one or more degrees higher than the note
bearing the shake' (I. 161).   He gives two examples, on
pp. 165–6 (Exx. 84–5).

Ex. 84   Partita IV, Menuet, bars 3–4.   OE

Ex. 85   Partita I, Allemande, bars 11–12.   OE

There is no eighteenth-century authority for beginning
such shakes as these on the main note.   On the contrary, there

is fairly convincing authority for beginning them on the auxiliary. Ex. 86a shows Marpurg 'blurring the melodic

Ex. 86   F. W. Marpurg, Anleitung, 1755 (Tab. IV, nos 30, 31)

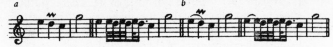

outline'; and his example agrees with one of Couperin's (1713, p. 74) in everything except that Marpurg's notation is precise, whereas Couperin's is not. Further evidence will be found in Agricola (pp. 64, 99f); and see Ex. 276. There is, in fact, no doubt that in Exx. 84–5 the shakes begin on the auxiliary in the ordinary way. In Ex. 85 one might even be tempted to prolong the auxiliary (Ex. 87).

Ex. 87   W.E.

In Ex. 88 it makes no difference whether the shake is played short or prolonged to the full length of the note; in either case, it will begin in the same way. It is instructive to compare this passage with Ex. 89.

Ex. 88   French Overture, Ouverture, bar 4.   OE

Ex. 89   French Overture, Courante, bars 10–11.   OE

By the ordinary rules of substitution, the appoggiatura in
Ex. 89 might be replaced by a short shake (⁓; see p. 112);
and the short shake would presumably be a Trillo, beginning
on the auxiliary (*b'*). Ex. 88 is similar in its general outline,
and it seems pretty certain that the shake, whether short or
long, begins on *e"*.

7. Dannreuther says (I. 165) that shakes in ascending
chains begin with the auxiliary. Türk gives Ex. 90 (where
the 'direct' specifies the beginning of the second shake), and
Quantz supports him; but this orthodox interpretation will

Ex. 90   Türk, p. 260

not always serve.   In Ex. 91 the consecutive octaves can no
doubt be disregarded, but not the fifths.

Ex. 91   Organ Sonata II. i. 68–9.   Autograph : orthodox interpretation

The following examples are not directly concerned with
Dannreuther, and are given here only as further illustrations
of the beginnings of shakes.

If there is any valid objection to an orthodox interpretation of Ex. 92, it is not so much that the melodic line is blurred

Ex. 92   WK II, Fugue in G sharp minor, bar 64.   Autograph

as that the legato is broken by the repetition of $\sharp d''$.   As the bass provides continuous quaver movement, one can tie the first note of the shake (Ex. 93).

Ex. 93   W.E.

Some players may find the orthodox interpretation in Ex. 94 satisfactory.   Others may like to try a Frescobaldian interpretation, or a prefix (Ex. 95).

Ex. 94   WK II, Prelude in E minor, bars 32–3.   Autograph

W.E.

Ex. 95   W.E.

8. Experience shows that it is necessary to mention those contexts in which the ornamented note is preceded by the same note. With rare exceptions, such as those mentioned in the footnote to p. 42, the shake begins on the auxiliary (Ex. 96). Shakes of this common type are often misinterpreted, especially by orchestral players.

Ex. 96   Brandenburg Concerto II. i. 9.   Autograph

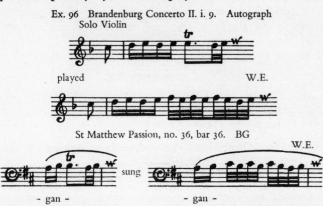

This discussion ends as it began, with the statement that the vast majority of Bach's 'plain' shakes begin on the auxiliary. There are exceptions—Ex. 65 is one, and it is not unique—but they are rare.*

* Kreutz (see p. 146) admits more numerous exceptions, and agrees, on the whole, fairly closely with Dannreuther. Two of his recommendations are worth noting here. Shakes on holding-notes, he says, should begin on the main note and end without closing-notes (e.g. Ex. 2); and in Exx. 76, 84 it seems that he would adopt Frescobaldian interpretations, such as those in Exx. 56, 95a.

The player who habitually begins shakes on the main note should ask himself whether he has any real reason for doing so. May it not be that he was badly taught as a child, and has grown accustomed to his own interpretations without ever giving any serious thought to them?

Prefixes

Prefixes are specified by ascending or descending hooks (☞ ☜). Some eighteenth-century copyists used small notes for this purpose (Ex. 97).* According to Türk, notations *a*, *b*, and *d* are slipshod, suggesting, as they do, the interpretations *f*, *g*, and *h*; besides, the single small note in *a* might be read as an appoggiatura. Only notations *c* and *e* are strictly in accordance with the 'rule' that all plain shakes begin on the auxiliary, and with the further 'rule', which Türk takes for granted, that prefixes are always of the types shown in Ex. 98.

Ex. 97   Türk and C.P.E.B.

Once again, one cannot help wondering how universal these 'rules' were. Notations *a* and *d* are quoted by Emanuel Bach as well as by Türk. Türk says they are wrong, but Emanuel does not. Türk himself uses something very like notation *d*, without comment, in Ex. 103. Moreover, a written-out shake of type *h* occurs in Murschhauser (Prototypon, Finale 7mi Toni, bar 33).

* In substance, Ex. 97 will be found in C.P.E.B., Trill, §§22, 27, and Türk, pp. 267, 269. Ex. *b* has been transposed to facilitate comparison with *a* and *c*; and other minor discrepancies between the two authors' notation have been ignored.

Sebastian Bach's own interpretations of prefixes will be found in the Explication; they are transcribed here for convenience (Ex. 98).

Ex. 98   Explication

Sometimes, no doubt, prefixes should be added to shakes that Bach indicated by 'plain' signs (cf. p. 38 and Ex. 95). On the whole, however, players will do well to disregard this possibility until they have had a good deal of experience; for the appropriate contexts cannot be defined with any precision. One thing is nevertheless clear: prefixes can only be used on fairly long notes. Six notes are enough to give the effect of a 'plain' shake; eight at least are necessary when there is a prefix, as will be seen.

Emanuel Bach has some puzzling remarks on this matter. He gives the interpretations of Ex. 99, in which the first

Ex. 99   C.P.E.B., Trill, §§22, 27

shake has two notes too many, and the second has four notes too many. He goes on to say that the descending shake contains more notes than any other shake: notes that are long enough for other shakes may therefore be too short to carry descending shakes. Further, in Ex. 240 his descending shake is again the longest ornament. It follows that the inaccurate notation of Ex. 99 must have a meaning of some kind.

There are no closing-notes in Ex. 99; but Emanuel probably had them at the back of his mind. Türk (pp. 267, 270) thought it 'almost superfluous' to specify closing-notes for shakes with prefixes; such shakes, he says, can only occur on fairly long notes, and players will therefore supply closing-notes instinctively. Bearing this in mind, one can make sense of Emanuel's remarks.

According to Sebastian Bach's Explication (nos 5 and 7), an ascending shake, with or without closing-notes, requires eight notes. This apparently did not give enough of the shake proper (enough repercussions, that is) to satisfy Emanuel, who, disregarding accuracy of notation, makes an ascending shake *without* closing-notes require ten notes.

As for the descending shake with closing-notes, if it had only eight notes it would consist simply of two turns, and could hardly be called a shake at all. Sebastian Bach saw this. His example in the Explication (no. 8) has twelve notes; but the main note is a dotted crotchet, and the notation is correct. Emanuel (Ex. 99) gives twelve notes to a descending shake *without* closing-notes, and incorrectly makes the main note a crotchet.

Doubts about the interpretation of these shakes arise in the usual way: when the first note of the prefix is preceded by the same note, or by a skip that seems to break the melodic line. It is likely, however, that shakes with prefixes should almost always be taken literally. For instance, Emanuel Bach says that ascending shakes can be used in the contexts of Ex. 100. He gives no interpretations; but neither does he give

Ex. 100   C.P.E.B., Trill, §25

special instructions. One can only conclude that in both cases he would have 'broken the melodic line': in the first, by repeating the c'', in the second, by skipping to it.

He does give one example of a tied interpretation (Ex. 101); unfortunately, without a word of explanation. This nevertheless justifies one in using a tie occasionally; and with prefixes, as with the shake in Ex. 92, a tie will sometimes prevent a certain feeling of awkwardness.

Ex. 101   C.P.E.B., Trill, §28

Ex. 101 and the Explication show that the prefix was generally thought of as beginning *on* the beat, not before it. In Ex. 102 the first notes seem to be a written-out descending prefix, and should probably be played as fast as the rest of the shake. Here again, the first note is tied.

Ex. 102   Organ Prelude in B minor, bars 67–8.   Autograph

In the time of Türk, however (1789), it was 'not unusual' for a prefix to be played before the beat, as in Ex. 103.

Ex. 103   Türk, p. 270

Türk considered this wrong; it came, he thought, from the Lombardic Style, in which appoggiaturas also were played before the beat, and thus converted into Nachschlags (p. 93). Be this as it may, Bach often wrote out ascending prefixes that come before the beat—for the common figuration of Ex. 4 amounts to nothing else—; and he sometimes treated descending prefixes in the same way (Exx. 104–6). Such prefixes can sometimes, though by no means always, be played faster than they are written; cf. Ex. 102.

Ex. 104   Organ Prelude in C, bar 19.   BG

Ex. 105   Gamba Sonata I, Andante, end.   BG

Ex. 106   Organ Sonata V. ii. 38.   Autograph

It is easy to argue that Bach wrote prefixes out whenever he meant them to be abnormal (*before* the beat), and used the ordinary signs (ᴄᴡ ᴄᴡ) when he meant the prefixes to be played in the 'ordinary' way (*on* the beat); but it does not take much experience of composers and their ways to make one realize that arguments of this kind are worthless.

Ex. 107 presents a pleasing problem. Should one take the

Ex. 107   WK II, Prelude in E minor, bars·28–9.   Autograph

notation literally, as at Ex. 108*a*: or as a hasty and inaccurate way of suggesting that the shake should begin on the main note (*b*): or as a Lombardic prefix, somewhat as in *c*? These are questions that each player must answer for himself.

Ex. 108
   a   *b*   *c*   W.E.

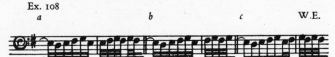

Appoggiatura Openings

Bach used two signs for appoggiatura openings: a vertical stroke attached to the shake sign, and a hook applied to the note (Ex. 109). These signs must not be confused with hooks attached to the shake sign (ᴄᴡ ᴄᴡ); the latter, as has been explained, stand for prefixes.

Ex. 100   Explication

The interpretation given by Bach in Ex. 109 is, of course, not strictly correct.

There is no satisfactory rule for the lengths of appoggiatura openings, any more than there is for ordinary appoggiaturas (see pp. 78ff). As with the latter, it is sensible to begin by playing appoggiatura openings short, and then see if they sound better when played longer. It is usually a matter of personal taste (Ex. 110).

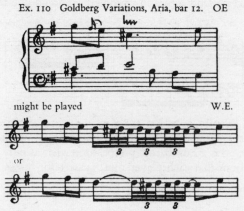

Ex. 110   Goldberg Variations, Aria, bar 12.   OE

might be played   W.E.

or

Interpretations of the second type (with a tie) are not shown in the Explication; but this does not prove that Bach did not use them (cf. p. 124). They are never necessary; but often permissible when, as in this case, there is movement in another part.

It is not impossible that the small note in Ex. 110 is a Nachschlag, and that the appoggiatura opening called for by the sign ∿ should be played as another Nachschlag—before the beat (Ex. 111). This depends on the player's attitude to the other small notes in this movement—for instance, those in Ex. 204.

Ex. 111   W.E.

Appoggiatura openings sometimes appear in unlikely-

looking contexts, such as that of Ex. 112. The awkwardness
that may be felt here cannot be avoided by tying the first
note as in Ex. 101; for this device cannot be applied to the
similar shakes at the beginning of the prelude, where there
are no other parts to keep the movement going. The awkwardness disappears with familiarity; but this does not prove
that the orthodox interpretation is right, for one can get
used to almost anything.

Ex. 112 XVIII, no. 2, *Komm, heiliger Geist*, bars 15–18. Autograph

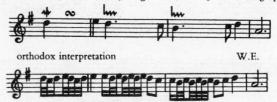

orthodox interpretation   W.E.

Ex. 112 gives the reading of the autograph.   Another
version of the prelude is known, of which there is no extant
autograph—only a copy made by Krebs, in which the ornamentation is supposed to be partly spurious. In this Krebs
MS, bars 15–18 are ornamented as in Ex. 113. The starred
ornament is a Nachschlag of the second type (p. 100). Its
authenticity is admittedly questionable; but it makes one
wonder whether the orthodox interpretation of Ex. 112 is
correct.

Ex. 113   Same as Ex. 112, from a Krebs MS quoted in BG

might be played   W.E.

Couperin and others seem to have begun most of their
shakes with appoggiaturas.   There is no justification for
applying their methods regularly to Bach; see p. 38.

Shakes covered by a slur

In such contexts as those of Exx. 114–5, the slur is treated
as a tie (cf. Exx. 42, 86). The closing-notes of Ex. 115 are
optional; that is to say, they are not specified by Bach's
notation. See p. 64.

Ex. 114   XVIII, no. 4, *Schmücke dich*, bar 29.   Autograph

Ex. 115   Orgelbüchlein, *Herr Gott*, bar 5.   Autograph

Closing-notes

The signs so far discussed (᪥ ᪥ *tr* ᪥ ᪥ ᪥) leave the
termination of the shake to the player's discretion; it is he
who must decide whether he will or will not use conventional closing-notes[*] (Exx. 91, 92, 115). Bach did, however,
use at least two methods of specifying closing-notes. Sometimes he wrote them out (Ex. 96); sometimes he added a
vertical stroke to the shake-sign (᪥, etc.; see the Explication).
Note that the vertical stroke signifying closing-notes comes
at the *end* of the sign.

[*] For unconventional closing-notes see Ex. 53 and p. 67.

One sometimes finds a descending hook at the end of a
shake sign (⤳ , etc., as in Ex. 119). Its meaning is uncertain, because one can seldom be sure whether the hook is
intentional, or due to an accidental flick of the pen.* It may
be a reminiscence of D'Anglebert's *Tremblement et pincé*
(Ex. 52, and cf. Ex. 259); and although it may not always
imply closing-notes, at any rate it is not always incompatible
with them (Ex. 116).

Ex. 116   WK II, Prelude in E minor, bar 77.   Autograph

Written-out closing-notes can sometimes be played
exactly as they are written (Ex. 96); but the notation is not
meant to be taken literally. It is determined by graphical
convenience: if a shake with written-out closing-notes is to
last for a crotchet, it is natural to write ♩♪ ; if for a
minim, ♩. ♪. In either case, the shake and its closing-
notes can be played in hemidemisemiquavers (♪) if it is
convenient to do so. Exx. 102 and 114 show closing-notes
that must certainly be played faster than Bach wrote them.

Emanuel Bach (Trill, §§14–15) says that closing-notes
should be as fast as the rest of the shake, and should run on
rapidly into the next note. This is a sound general rule.
Occasionally, however, the shake seems to run more smoothly
into its context if its closing-notes are played slowly. Compare the two interpretations of Ex. 117.

Ex. 117   Orgelbüchlein, *O Mensch*, bar 15.   Autograph

* See the reproductions, p. 150, nos 10–11.

Even when closing-notes are not specified, either by the vertical stroke or by being written out, they ought often to be added by the player (Exx. 91, 92, 115). Emanuel Bach deals with this matter at some length (Trill, §§13–18); the following notes record only the more straightforward of his recommendations.

If the ornamented note is short, closing-notes can be added in the context of Ex. 118a, but should not be used in b.

Ex. 118   C.P.E.B., Trill, §13

If the ornamented note is long, closing-notes are always permissible—even in Ex. 118b.   They can therefore be used in Ex. 119. Note the hook at the end of the sign.

Ex. 119   WK II, Prelude in A minor, bar 16.   Autograph

When a shake is followed by short notes that give something like the effect of closing-notes (Ex. 53), it is permissible, but not necessary, to use normal closing-notes as well.

Emanuel's further discussion of this matter is not at all clear; but he seems to mean that in such contexts as those of Ex. 53, if normal closing-notes are *not* used, the shake should run on into the substitute-notes (Ex. 120); whereas if normal closing-notes *are* used, there should be a slight break between them and the substitute-notes (Ex. 121). See also Ex. 131.

Ex. 120 Goldberg Variations, no. 16, bar 8. OE

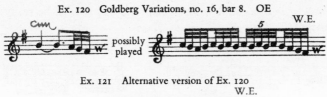

possibly
played

Ex. 121 Alternative version of Ex. 120

Shakes tied over

Shakes tied over a bar-line are usually stopped just before
the bar, so that the effect of the tie is felt. Closing-notes are
sometimes appropriate (Exx. 122–3).

Ex. 122 WK II, Prelude in E minor, bars 36–7. Autograph

Ex. 123 Italian Concerto i. 114–5. OE

There may, however, be authority for running tied shakes
on over the bar-line (Ex. 124). Emanuel's notation is not

E

as clear as one could wish; perhaps Ex. 125 is what he really
meant.

Ex. 124   C.P.E.B., Trill, §24   Ex. 125   W.E.

See also *Groppo*, p. 117.

Closing-notes in chains of shakes

In rising chains (Ex. 91) closing-notes can be added to all
the shakes, or to the last one only, at the player's discretion.
In Ex. 102 Bach specified them.

It is fortunate that descending chains are rare, for it is
exceedingly difficult to know how to treat them.   Ex. 126

Ex. 126   Organ Sonata IV. ii. 38.   Autograph

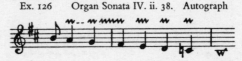

reproduces the notation of the autograph as closely as possible; but there is no doubt that Bach would have written
a continuous wavy line if the layout of the MS had made it
possible to do so.   The strictly legitimate interpretation is
given in Ex. 127*a*; but as the shakes are long, closing-notes
are permissible (*b*)—it may be thought that they provide a

Ex. 127
    a   *b*   W.E.

better approach to the repetition at the beginning of each
shake.   There are three ways of avoiding this repetition.
The first, for which there is not much to be said, is to tie the
last note of each shake to the first note of the next.   The
second is to begin alternate shakes on the main note.   The

third is to end the shakes on the upper or lower auxiliary (Ex. 128). A shake of the type shown in Ex. 128*b* will be

Ex. 128   W.E.

found in Murschhauser (Prototypon, Finale 7mi Toni, bar 33), and type *c* occurs in Partita II, Sinfonia, bar 29, and English Suite VI, Prelude, bar 47, etc.; these abnormal endings are therefore not altogether without authority.

Other terminations

It is commonly said that a shake on a dotted note stops at or near the dot. Taken at its face value, this 'rule' is more often wrong than right (see Exx. 83, 92, 96). In fact, there is only one type of context—admittedly a common one—in which it is applicable; and that is when the dotted note is followed by a single note, the latter being an unaccented anticipation (Exx. 129–31). In such cases the shake may stop at the dot if the tempo is at all fast (Exx. 129–30); but in slower tempi it is often effective to shorten the anticipation, and prolong the shake as if the main note were double-dotted (Ex. 131). A very short rest before the anticipation (as at the point marked by an arrow) may sometimes be effective.

Ex. 129   Brandenburg Concerto III. i. 77, Violin II.   Autograph
W.E.

Ex. 130   B minor Mass, Sanctus, end.   Trumpet I, sounding notes
Autograph   W.E.

played

Ex. 131   Partita I, Sarabande, bar 11.   OE
                                                    W.E.

played

or

Türk (p. 259) does not allow closing-notes in figuration
of this type, either ascending or descending. No doubt they
would be wrong in Ex. 130 (descending); but they might
be used on a long note with ascending figuration (Ex. 131).

Ex. 132 shows a special case: a shake on a dotted note,
separated by a rest from normal closing-notes. The passage
can be played somewhat as in Ex. 133. It is generally agreed
that the Overture style calls for double-dotting; but in this
case Bach may have meant the pairs of short notes in the
bass to be played as written.

Similar shakes occur in WK I, Prelude in E minor, bars
10 and 12.

Ex. 132   French Overture, Ouverture, bar 8.   OE

Ex. 133. W.E.

This example shows, as well as any, that eighteenth-century composers had excellent reasons for not writing ornaments out in full. It was not that they were indulging in deliberate mystification, or that they thought the ornaments unimportant; it was simply that Ex. 132 was much easier to write and read than Ex. 133, and showed up the melodic and harmonic framework much more clearly.

Short Shakes

It has been pointed out (p. 36) that Bach's shake signs are often ambiguous. A wavy line, appearing in a modern edition as ⁓, may very well mean a long shake. Players must be alive to this possibility, for a short shake can ruin such a passage as Ex. 114. Nevertheless, the sign ⁓ often does mean a short shake—one that occupies only part of the length of the ornamented note.

From its names to its interpretations, almost everything to do with the sign ⁓ is confused and highly controversial. The evidence for the following assertions and recommendations is discussed in Appendix I and on p. 147.

Four kinds of short shakes are described in eighteenth-century writings (Exx. 134–7).

No. 1 of the Explication is a Trillo, and no. 12 shows a slightly prolonged Imperfect Shake combined with an appoggiatura; thus, these two forms of short shake are authenticated. Bach undoubtedly used the Schneller also, and most probably the Pralltriller; but players should be a little cautious with these two forms: with the latter because there is no absolute proof that Bach used it, and with the former because there is a tendency to use it too often, at the expense of the Trillo.

The following examples have been classified for convenience.

WHEN THE ORNAMENTED NOTE IS PRECEDED BY THE SAME NOTE

In vigorous movements the ornament will be either a Trillo or a Schneller (Exx. 138–9, 280).

Ex. 138 Brandenburg Concerto II. iii. 1. Autograph
Allegro assai
Trumpet, sounding notes

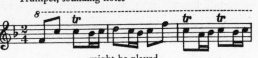

might be played

Schneller   W.E.

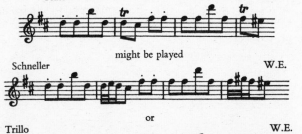

Ex. 139 Orchestral Suite II, Badinerie, bar 7. Peters Urtext edition
Flute

might be played

Schneller   W.E.

or

Trillo   W.E.

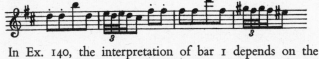

In Ex. 140, the interpretation of bar 1 depends on the
player's view of the relationship between bar 1 and bar 9.
If bar 9 is to be regarded as a parallel, the shake in bar 1 will

Ex. 140 Partita III, Burlesca. OE

bar 1   Schneller   W.E.

played

bar 9

be long, and the semiquavers will become normal closing-notes; but if bar 9 is a mere veiled allusion, there is something to be said for the jerky accented effect of a Schneller in bar 1.

In slow movements a Trillo is often effective (Ex. 141).

Ex. 141   Organ Sonata III. ii. 8.   Autograph

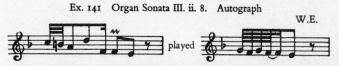

played

In Ex. 142 the ornamentation is varied at the repeat. The appoggiatura in bar 5 strongly suggests that the ornament in bar 29 should be a Trillo, beginning on *a'*; cf. Ex. 49. Nevertheless, this suggestive parallelism does not amount to proof; see Exx. 240–1.

Ex. 142   XVIII, no. 9, *Nun komm.*   Autograph

WHEN THE ORNAMENTED NOTE IS TIED

Only one interpretation seems possible (Ex. 143).

Ex. 143   Organ Sonata III. i. 1.   Autograph

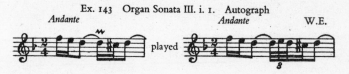

played

WHEN THE PREVIOUS NOTE IS A STEP HIGHER
THAN THE ORNAMENTED NOTE

Previous note accented

It seems rather unlikely that the shakes in Ex. 144 should be played as Trillos, for the Trillo gives a certain effect of

Ex. 144 Organ Sonata I. i. Autograph

bar 2

accent that would be inappropriate here (Ex. 145). A Pralltriller would serve in bar 4 (Ex. 146), but not in bar 2,

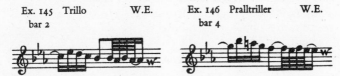

Ex. 145 Trillo   W.E.   Ex. 146 Pralltriller   W.E.
bar 2   bar 4

where the other parts do not move on the fourth quaver.
As the two bars must agree, those who dislike a Trillo must
play an Imperfect Shake (Ex. 147).

Ex. 147 Imperfect Shake   W.E.
bar 2

Previous note accented and slurred

The slur is usually treated as a tie, so that the ornament
becomes a Pralltriller (see the *second* shake in Ex. 148).

Ex. 148 Orgelbüchlein, *Das alte Jahr*, bar 6. Autograph

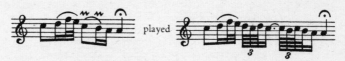

When there is no movement in the other parts, however, the Imperfect Shake of Ex. 149 is preferable.

Ex. 149 Partita IV, Sarabande, bar 1. OE

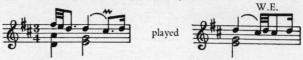

Main note accented

Any kind of short shake may be right, according to the strength of the accent. In Ex. 88 a Trillo is perhaps safest: in Ex. 279, Pralltrillers and an Imperfect Shake. A Schneller is most probably right in Ex. 150, where the short shakes are directly opposed to mordents; see the more extended quotation in Ex. 10, and the remarks on pp. 140–1.

Ex. 150 French Overture, Gigue, bars 3–4. OE

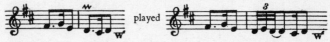

In Ex. 151 a Trillo is practically unplayable at any reasonable tempo. As there is movement in another part, players who hesitate to use a Schneller can adopt a tied interpretation.

Ex. 151 Organ Sonata V. iii. 4. Autograph

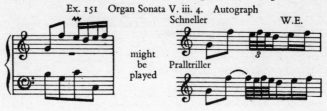

Main note accented and slurred to the previous note

Clearly the slur in Ex. 152 cannot possibly be treated as a tie. The ornament must be a Schneller, beginning on the beat and with the main note.

Ex. 152 Duetto IV, bar 18. OE

WHEN THE PREVIOUS NOTE IS A THIRD HIGHER
THAN THE ORNAMENTED NOTE

The ornament is a Trillo (Ex. 153).

Ex. 153 French Overture, Gigue, bars 11–12. OE

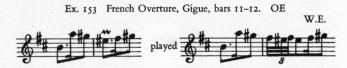

WHEN THE PREVIOUS NOTE IS MORE THAN A THIRD
HIGHER THAN THE ORNAMENTED NOTE

The ornament is probably a Trillo. Compare Ex. 154 with the parallel Ex. 155. Admittedly, the appoggiatura in bar 18 does not prove that the short shake in bar 161 ought to begin with the auxiliary; but it is highly suggestive. See on the one hand Ex. 142, and on the other Exx. 240–1.

Ex. 154 French Overture, Ouverture, bars 160–1. OE

Ex. 155 The same, bars 17–18

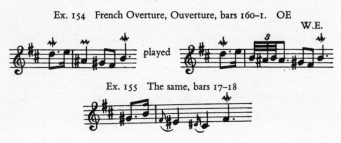

WHEN THE SIGN ⌒ IS PRECEDED BY AN
APPOGGIATURA SIGN

The appoggiatura sign may be either a hook or a small note (see the next chapter). In Ex. 156 it happens to be a hook. As a rule, its length is a matter for the player to decide.

Ex. 156   Orgelbüchlein, *Wenn wir*, bar 6.   Autograph

The ⌒ is here interpreted as an Imperfect Shake, in accordance with the Explication. If there had been movement in another part, it might have been a Pralltriller; but when an appoggiatura is combined with a shake, one seldom finds movement elsewhere. See p. 125.

THE APPOGGIATURA

BACH indicated appoggiaturas by small notes (usually quavers or semiquavers), and also by single or double hooks (⌣ ϛ). The double-hook sign has no separate meaning; the second of the two hooks seems to be nothing more than the slur that is conventionally attached to appoggiaturas in print and in careful writing; see Ex. 189. In the original manuscripts, the hook signs are often misplaced.

As the hooks have been translated into small notes by all but the most conscientious editors, it is impossible to say, without access to large numbers of autograph manuscripts, whether Bach made any distinction between hooks and small notes. If the BG is to be trusted, he used them indifferently in the tenor aria of Cantata 67 (BG XVI. 228). It is true that

* In the Complete Autograph Bach wrote

Dannreuther thought he saw 'some delicate distinction' in bar 11, and suggested that the hook might stand for a Nachschlag (type I); but this seems extremely unlikely. The hook in bar 11 must surely have the same meaning as the small note in the parallel bar 21 (Ex. 157). One can see, however, that when an appoggiatura required an accidental, Bach preferred a small note to a hook. See also Ex. 190.

Ex. 157 Cantata 67, tenor aria. BG

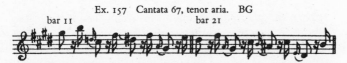

In J. S. Bach's music, so far as is known, the length of the small note has nothing to do with the length of the appoggiatura. In Ex. 183, for instance, Dolmetsch reasonably interprets a small quaver as a dotted crotchet; see also Exx. 178–9.

Bach did not use the sign ♪. It appears occasionally in modern editions, and even in the BG (St Matthew Passion, p. 208, etc.); but it is always wrong, and should be replaced by the ordinary appoggiatura sign.

It is possible that some of the rising appoggiaturas in modern editions ought to be replaced by Slides; see p. 30.

Small notes and single hooks stand for Nachschlags as well as for appoggiaturas, and it is rather unlikely that Nachschlags of Type I (p. 93) are as rare as they are supposed to be. If the small notes in Ex. 158 are played *on* the beat, as appoggiaturas, they make consecutives at the stars. They must therefore be played *before* the beat, as Nachschlags. See p. 95.

Ex. 158 Goldberg Variations, no. 13, bar 17. OE

Canonic Variations, Canon at the Seventh, bars 16–17. OE

When the player has made up his mind that a small note or hook is an appoggiatura, and not a Nachschlag, he has still to determine its length. Sometimes, as in Ex. 159, this matter is settled beyond all question by the context; but such cases are rare.

Ex. 159 Cantata 67, tenor aria, bar 8. BG

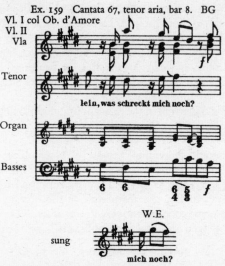

There is only one clear rule about the length of appoggiaturas: that given by Quantz (p. 79):

'When there is a shake on a note that is discordant with the bass*—an augmented fourth, diminished fifth,

---

* It will be observed that although Quantz speaks of shakes on notes that are discordant with the bass, in his examples *b* and *c* the shakes are on the bass notes themselves.

seventh, or second—the appoggiatura before the shake must be quite short, so that the discord shall not be turned into a concord. For instance, if the appoggiatura *a'* in [Ex. 160*c*] were held half as long as the following ♯*g'*, on which there is a shake, one would hear a sixth (*f"* to *a'*) instead of a seventh (*f"* to ♯*g'*); that is to say, there would be no discord.'

Ex. 160   Quantz

This agrees with Emanuel Bach's more limited statement (Appoggiatura, §14): 'When the appoggiatura makes a perfect octave with the bass, it cannot be long, for the harmony would sound too empty.'

The only discords actually mentioned by Quantz are the augmented fourth, diminished fifth, seventh, and second. It is obvious, however, that these discords can be implied by other intervals—for instance, in Ex. 167 the ornamented notes in bar 2 both imply seconds, although they are *perfect* fourths. It follows that whenever an appoggiatura is consonant with its accompanying parts, it must be short.

This rule must always be borne in mind; for although it seldom shows that an appoggiatura must be of a certain definite length, it often gives a definite maximum value. Besides, apart from it there is no rule at all—nothing but a list of possibilities, authenticated after a fashion by various authors who may—or may not—have agreed with Bach. The player must select that possibility which seems to him most sensible, remembering that the Explication is worthless so far as appoggiaturas are concerned.

When one is sight-reading, or just beginning to give serious attention to the ornamentation of a piece one is learning, it is not a bad plan to play all appoggiaturas short—at the very most a quarter of the main note, or a sixth if the main note is dotted. Later, one should experiment with longer interpretations, giving due attention to consistency.

Rising and falling appoggiaturas are treated in exactly the same way.

An appoggiatura *may* take as much as half the value of the main note: or one third, or even two thirds, if the main note is dotted.

Organ Fantasia in C minor

In the autograph (cf. the facsimile in BG XLIV) this work is very heavily ornamented, and begins as in Ex. 161.

Ex. 161   Autograph

The appoggiatura in bar 1, the corresponding one in the alto of bar 2, and those in all the later entries of the subject, can be played as quavers; but obviously they cannot be longer than quavers.

By Quantz's Rule, the appoggiatura in bar 3 must be shorter than a crotchet, to preserve the discord (the seventh, $\flat a'$ to g''). The longest reasonable interpretation is a quaver. This appoggiatura answers that in the upper part of bar 2; and it is manifestly undesirable to obscure this fact by interpreting them in different ways. Accordingly, the first appoggiatura in bar 2 must be at most a quaver, although under Possibility I it might have been a crotchet.

These four appoggiaturas, and the parallel ones that occur later, can be played as quavers (Ex. 162). This interpretation

Ex. 162 W.E

fills up a number of gaps in the quaver movement, and is perhaps further justified by the allusions to the subject at the stars in bars 64–5 (Ex. 163), where Bach used ordinary notation.

Ex. 163 The same, bars 64–5

The appoggiaturas in bar 12 should no doubt be longer (Ex. 184), and those in the manual parts of bars 25, 27, 29 shorter. As they are not parallel with those in bars 1–3, there is no need to interpret them in the same way.

French Overture, Sarabande, central cadence

The engraver of the original edition went wrong here, and in the end Bach left the passage only half corrected. His intentions are nevertheless clear (Ex. 164). If one plays the

Ex. 164 OE, emended
bar 12

repeat, it is effective to vary the treatment of the appoggiaturas, as in Ex. 165. See also Ex. 244.

Ex. 165   W.E.

Organ Prelude in B minor

In Ex. 166, the quaver interpretation permitted by Possibility I is forbidden by Quantz's Rule.

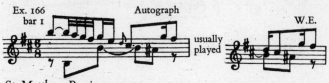

St Matthew Passion, no. 33

According to Quantz's Rule, the second and third appoggiaturas in Ex. 167 cannot be quavers; and this means that none of them can be, for obviously they must all be treated alike.

Ex. 167   bar 1   Autograph

Dolmetsch suggests crotchets; but this interpretation also seems to be forbidden by Quantz's Rule, and it certainly implies very strange harmony (Ex. 168). Perhaps these appoggiaturas should all be semiquavers (Ex. 169).

Ex. 168   Dolmetsch

Ex. 169   W.E.

Orchestral Suite in B minor, Menuet

Ex. 170   BG and Peters Urtext
bar 9

The appoggiatura can be as short as a semiquaver, or (according to Possibility I) as long as a minim. Before coming to a decision, one must examine the parallel passages in the movement; see Ex. 172.

POSSIBILITY II

An appoggiatura on a tied note *may* take the whole value
of the note.

WK II, Prelude in C sharp minor

In this slow smooth movement one can take advantage of
Possibility II, and adopt the interpretations shown. There is
no autograph of this Prelude and Fugue; but the text of the
passages quoted is satisfactorily established.

Orchestral Suite in B minor, Menuet

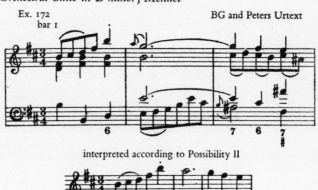

It is obviously unlikely that the appoggiatura in bar 2 takes the whole value of its main note according to Possibility II, if only because that interpretation would obscure the connection between this appoggiatura and those in bar 10, etc. (Ex. 170), which cannot be treated in this way. In bar 2 the minim interpretation seems rhythmically weak; moreover, one feels that this appoggiatura ought to match that in bar 3. As the latter can hardly be anything but a semiquaver, there is justification for playing all the appoggiaturas in this movement as semiquavers.

French Overture, Gigue

According to Quantz (p. 79, §9), Possibility II is appropriate in gigues; and some may feel that this sufficiently justifies Ex. 173. Elsewhere in this movement, however,

Ex. 173   OE

according to Quantz

mordents and short shakes are frequently used as accents (Ex. 10); and it can be argued that Bach meant the appoggiaturas to produce a similar effect. If so, they must be short, somewhat as in Ex. 174.

Ex. 174   W.E.

F

French Overture, Bourrée II

There are five appoggiaturas in this movement (bars 1, 2, 21, 22, and 24); and Possibility II can be applied to the first four, but not to the last one. Bars 1 and 2 are more or less parallel with bars 21 and 22; and the interpretation of these four ornaments is governed by the player's attitude to the passage quoted in Ex. 175. The appoggiatura in bar 24 can

Ex. 175   OE

hardly be longer than a quaver, and is probably better as a semiquaver. Does the lie of the passage demand that the three appoggiaturas should be the same (Ex. 176), or is it better that they should be different (Ex. 177)?

Ex. 176   W.E.

Organ Prelude in B minor

The three passages are more or less parallel; but in the first
Bach wrote a quaver appoggiatura, in the second a semiquaver, and in the third, none.

The first question is, whether Bach did or did not mean
an appoggiatura to be played in bar 34. This has to be
answered by a purely musical judgement, and therefore by
the player himself. He must remember that Bach did sometimes omit necessary ornaments, and that as this appoggiatura
is in the Berlin MS P 290, it cannot be dismissed as altogether
foreign to eighteenth-century habits of thought.

The player who decides to add an appoggiatura in bar 34
will find that the likeliest interpretations are a dotted crotchet
(Possibility II: see Ex. 181) and a demisemiquaver (Ex. 182).
Either of these will serve in bars 8 and 10 also; and all three
passages will, of course, be played in the same way.

Ex. 181   W.E.

Ex. 182   W.F.

The player who decides not to add an appoggiatura in bar 34 can consider bars 8 and 10 by themselves, and has a wider choice of interpretations. These appoggiaturas can be dotted crotchets (Possibility II), quavers, semiquavers, or demisemiquavers; it may even be that the first ought to be a quaver and the second a semiquaver, exactly as Bach wrote them.

POSSIBILITY III

When the main note is followed by a rest, the appoggiatura *may* take the whole value of the main note.

WK II, Prelude in E flat

Ex. 183   Autograph
   bar 1

played   W.E.

This interpretation, on the lines suggested by Dolmetsch, is quite satisfactory; the only reasonable alternative is a quaver.

Organ Fantasia in C minor

Ex. 184
bar 11   Autograph

Like most of the appoggiaturas in this movement, those in
bar 11 can be played as quavers (cf. Ex. 161). Those in bar 12
are better as crotchets. If they are made minims, in accordance
with Possibility III, the rest has to be cut short, and its effect
is weakened.

St Matthew Passion, no. 36

At the end of the second choral passage, the original First
Violin part has Ex. 185. Possibility III would call for the
interpretation of Ex. 186; but the autograph full score has
Ex. 187, and comparison with the ends of the other sections
in this movement leaves one in no doubt that Ex. 187 is right.

Ex. 185   Autograph Part, from Schneider's edition

Ex. 186   W.E.   Ex. 187   Autograph Score

Organ Sonata VI. iii. 18

Ex. 188   Autograph

Clearly Possibility III cannot apply here; the appoggiatura cannot be longer than a quaver.

Cantata 67, tenor aria

For another passage in which Possibility III cannot apply, see Ex. 159.

WK II, Prelude in G sharp minor

Ex. 189 bar 2   Autograph

This is an instructive example, in more ways than one.

Firstly, Possibility III is, once again, obviously out of the question.

Secondly, in the parallel passages* Bach sometimes wrote single and sometimes double hooks. There is no doubt that the second hook is simply the conventional slur.

Thirdly, in this movement as in Ex. 157, Bach used hooks only when the ornaments were diatonic. In bars 44–5 (Ex. 190), where they required accidentals, he used notes: in this case ordinary notes, instead of the small notes of Ex. 157.

Ex. 190   bar 44   Autograph

The appoggiaturas in bar 2 and the parallel passages cannot be longer than quavers; and this, the longest, is also the most

* See the reproduction, p. 150, no. 13.

natural interpretation. Dolmetsch, however, goes too far
when he cites bars 44–5 as 'a positive proof that this is right',
saying that Bach wrote these bars in ordinary notation
because he could not have expressed his intentions by using
appoggiaturas. Appoggiatura notation, with small notes,
would have done perfectly well, as Ex. 191 shows. If anyone

Ex. 191   bar 44   W.E.

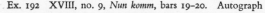

were so perversely inclined, he could argue that, just because
Bach used ordinary quavers in bars 44–5, he must have meant
something else in bar 2.

APPOGGIATURAS MOVING BY SKIP

THE appoggiaturas discussed in the last chapter are ordinary
ones, moving upwards or downwards, but always by step.
There is another type of ornament that is indicated by a
small note, but moves by skip. No doubt it ought to have
a separate name; but it does not seem to have been given one,
presumably because it is treated as if it were a rather short
appoggiatura. It is mentioned in Marpurg (1749), p. 66.

    This ornament is not very common, and Exx. 192–6 will
illustrate it sufficiently.

Ex. 192   XVIII, no. 9, *Nun komm*, bars 19-20. Autograph

Ex. 193   Organ Prelude in E flat, bars 44–5.   OE

[senza Ped.]

Ex. 194   Goldberg Variations, no. 25, bar 13.   OE

Ex. 195   Three-part Invention in E flat, bars 5–7.   Autograph (1723)

Ex. 196   Suite in A for Clavier and Violin, Courante, bar 88.   BG

Ex. 197, a passage parallel to Ex. 194, provides a clue to the

Ex. 197   Goldberg Variations, no. 25, bar 21.   OE

interpretation of these ornaments.   It is reasonable to play them all on the beat, and to give the small notes the following values: Ex. 192, semiquaver: Ex. 193, quaver: Ex. 194, semiquaver: Ex. 195, semiquaver: Ex. 196, quaver.   Thus, Ex. 192 can be played as in Ex. 198.

Ex. 198   W.E.

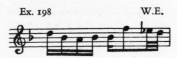

THE NACHSCHLAG

THERE are two ornaments called Nachschlag.   The first moves by step, and is indicated by a small note or a hook; the second moves by skip, and is indicated by a small note. They are both played *off* the beat.   Typical interpretations, based on Emanuel Bach, are given in Exx. 199-200.

Ex. 199   Type I   W.E.

Ex. 200   Type II   W.E.

played

Type I can be further subdivided, according to whether the ornament forms part of a descending scale (Ex. 201), or occurs between tied or repeated notes (Exx. 27, 158, 206). In the latter case it can be called *Rückschlag*; but the distinction seems rather pointless, and is not observed in this book. Type II is sometimes called *Überschlag* or *Überwurf*.

It has often been said that Emanuel's violent objection to Nachschlags of either type is purely personal, and has nothing to do with his father's music. Much more to the point is Mitchell's remark, that Emanuel's fulminations were directed primarily at people who played Nachschlags where appoggiaturas were intended (in the Lombardic Style; see p. 58), and added Nachschlags where ornaments were not necessary. Emanuel has nevertheless left his mark on twentieth-century interpretations: it is still considered good form to regard all his father's hooks and small notes as appoggiaturas unless the context proves beyond all question that they are Nachschlags. It is very doubtful whether there is any justification for this attitude.

TYPE I

The chief difficulty with Nachschlags of Type I is to identify them, since, so far as notation goes, they are indistinguishable from appoggiaturas. There are two hints that may be useful. If a hook or small note resolves upwards, it is certainly an appoggiatura. On the other hand, if in a series of falling thirds (Ex. 199) there are two or more hooks or small notes, there is a fair chance that they are Nachschlags.*

Ex. 201 is a clear case of a Type I Nachschlag. The appoggiatura interpretation is harmonically highly improbable. See also the first bars of this prelude (Ex. 29).

* A fair chance, but nothing more. It must be clearly understood that Nachschlags are not obligatory in this context. Compare bars 12 and 23 in the Schübler chorale prelude on *Meine Seele*. The context is that of Ex. 199; but the small notes are appoggiaturas.

Ex. 201   XVIII, no. 12, *Allein Gott*, bar 26.   Autograph

played   W.E.

The passages quoted in Ex. 158 are even clearer cases, since consecutives can only be avoided by playing the ornaments as Nachschlags. As a rule, however, there is room for differences of opinion.

Dolmetsch sees Nachschlags in Ex. 202. The figuration resembles that of Ex. 29 so closely that he may well be right;

Ex. 202   WK II, Prelude in B, bars 23-4.   Autograph

played   W.E.

not this

but only if the Slide (which he omits) is played before the beat. If it is played on the beat, the hooks are better as appoggiaturas (Ex. 203).

Ex. 203   W.E.

In Ex. 204 Dolmetsch sees one Nachschlag, and Dannreuther two; but the appoggiaturas recommended in Kirk-

Ex. 204   Goldberg Variations, Aria, bar 2   OE

OE   Dolmetsch   Dannreuther   Kirkpatrick

patrick's edition are equally satisfactory as harmony. Landowska, in her recording, plays both the small notes as semiquaver appoggiaturas. Players must not come to any conclusion about this bar without examining all the parallel passages in the Aria; see, for instance, Ex. 110.

Of the other examples quoted by Dannreuther, no doubt Ex. 205 contains Nachschlags; so also, most probably,

Ex. 205   Suite in A for Clavier and Violin, Courante, bar 92.   BG

Ex. 105. Ex. 206 seems rather doubtful: the question being not so much whether Bach meant a Nachschlag or an appoggiatura as whether he really meant anything at all. The ornament does not occur in any of the parallel passages; and it cannot be added consistently by the player, for in the first of the parallels (bars 14-15) it would make consecutive

perfect fifths.   The consecutives made by a Nachschlag in
Ex. 206 are probably permissible (Mitchell, p. 200, §22).

Ex. 206   Gamba Sonata I, Finale, bars 6–7.   BG

The small note in Ex. 27 has been interpreted as a Nachschlag, to draw attention to a possibility that seems to have
been ignored hitherto.   See also the Triple Concerto (for
Flute, Violin, and Clavier: BWV1044), at bar 12 of the slow
movement.

Landshoff sees Nachschlags in Ex. 207, and also in bar 34,
which is not quoted here.   He bases this interpretation on

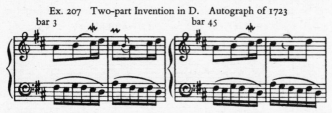

Ex. 207   Two-part Invention in D.   Autograph of 1723
bar 3   bar 45

the earlier autograph, in which bar 46 is written out in full
(Ex. 208).   Landshoff's opinions are not to be taken lightly;

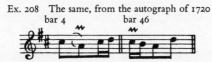

Ex. 208   The same, from the autograph of 1720
bar 4   bar 46

but the fact remains that the large-note figuration of bar 46
is not parallel with that of bar 4, and the ornamentation in
the autograph of 1723 is not the same as that in the autograph
of 1720.   Here—as usual—the player must suit himself.

In Ex. 209 the brass and voice parts are irrelevant, and
have been omitted.   If the first violin part stood alone, one

would naturally take the small note for an appoggiatura, and

Ex. 209   Christmas Oratorio, last movement of Part IV, bars 13-14.   BG

play it, probably, as a crotchet; but if the violin is to double
the first oboe part—and surely it must—the small note has
to be played as a Nachschlag. This raises doubts about the
small note in bar 5 of the same movement (Ex. 210).

Ex. 210   The same, bars 5-6

When the conductor has made up his mind whether the
small notes are Nachschlags or appoggiaturas, he has still to
settle the treatment of the shake in bar 13. Taking into consideration all three of the instruments that play it, is it not
most reasonable to begin with the main note?

The interesting and very unusual piece of notation in
Ex. 211 is probably authentic, for although there is no extant

autograph, it appears in all six of the manuscripts on which

Ex. 211   Organ Fugue in E minor (Wedge), bar 32. From MS P 274

the BG text is based, and in a seventh that was not used for that edition. It has hitherto been successfully concealed by the nineteenth-century editors of Bach's organ works, who printed it in the following forms (Ex. 212). The first small

Ex. 212   Various editions

note seems to be a Nachschlag, the second an appoggiatura; and the second version in Ex. 212 is, no doubt, a reasonable interpretation. The alternative (♩.♩♪.) seems out of keeping.

Ex. 211, and its faithful reproduction in seven manuscripts, throws light on an otherwise plausible interpretation by David in his edition of the early (C minor) version of the French Overture. David suggests that the right-hand part of bar 5 should be played as in Ex. 213.

Ex. 213   Interpretation by David
bar 5

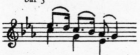

What Bach originally wrote will never be known, for the autograph has disappeared; but if he had meant this, he would have used one of the notations given in Ex. 214. The notation

Ex. 214   W.E.

actually used in his wife's careful copy, on which David's edition is based, is given in Ex. 215; and the original edition agrees with Ex. 215 in all essentials.

Ex. 215   French Overture, Ouverture, bar 5.   A. M. Bach's MS (P 226)

The first notation in Ex. 214 is strikingly unlike that of Ex. 215; and the second notation, like that of Ex. 211, is so unusual that one would expect it to have been reproduced correctly. Thus, if Bach had used either of the notations given in Ex. 214, it is hardly credible that his wife and the engravers should have misrepresented his intentions to the extent of Ex. 215. It follows that David's added Nachschlag —the ♭b' in Ex. 213—is unjustifiable; there are only two ornaments in this passage, and they are both appoggiaturas.

TYPE II

Nachschlags of Type II (Ex. 200) occasionally appear in modern editions, as for instance in Ex. 216. They are probably corruptions due to late eighteenth-century copyists. The ornament was common enough in 1753 to call forth outspoken comment from Emanuel Bach; but there does not seem to be any evidence that his father used it. The interpretation of Ex. 200 is satisfactory.

Ex. 216   Organ Trio in D minor, bar 12.   Peters

The manuscript source of Ex. 216 is not available; but one may suppose that the Peters editor replaced an ordinary small note by the sign ♪.

THE sign for this ornament consists of two small notes. It is rare in Bach; indeed, only one example is given by Dannreuther and Dolmetsch, and this is not autograph (Ex. 217).

Ex. 217   Sarabande in F minor, bars 4–5.   BG

Two others occur in a non-autograph manuscript of the organ Prelude in B minor (Berlin MS P 290).

From Emanuel Bach and others one gathers that the Anschlag should be played as shown, with the main note louder than the small notes. Similar figuration occurs, fully written out, at the stars in Ex. 218.

Ex. 218   Goldberg Variations, no. 25.   OE

THE ARPEGGIO

SOME of Bach's contemporaries used the signs ⌇ and ⌇, (or L and Γ), meaning respectively 'spread upwards' and 'spread downwards'. Bach may have used these signs; but there is no unmistakable example of them in the autographs I have seen, and it is certain that he was often content to use the wavy line ⌇ that is familiar today.

The sign } can always be interpreted in the usual modern way, by spreading the chord rapidly upwards; but a downward interpretation sometimes helps to clarify the melodic line. In his edition, Kirkpatrick interprets Ex. 219 as shown; and Landowska's version, in her recording, is almost the same. On long notes there seems no reason why the chord should not be spread in both directions (cf. Ex. 236).

Ex. 219   Goldberg Variations, Aria, bars 10-11.   OE   Kirkpatrick

On the harpsichord or clavichord, a chord is often very much more effective when spread than when played *sec.* On the piano, wholesale arpeggiation of chords would no doubt be a mistake; but the possibility should be borne in mind by anyone who has access to the original instruments, and is sometimes helpful even on the piano.

As Dolmetsch remarks, Bach almost certainly meant the chords in Ex. 220 to be spread; and here it is most decidedly

Ex. 220   WK I, Prelude in B flat, fragments of bars 15-18. BG (Bischoff)

advantageous to adopt abnormal forms of arpeggiation, to bring out the part-writing. The first interpretation in Ex. 221 is borrowed from Dolmetsch, and can hardly be improved on. The rest may be thought illegitimate; but they are put forward only as suggestions. Nothing more is claimed for them than that they have been tried on a clavichord. The notation is approximate, the position of the beats being shown by the accents.

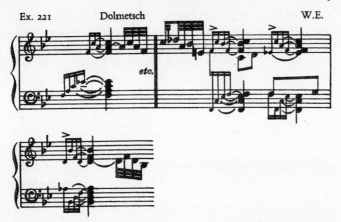

Ex. 221   Dolmetsch   W.E.

It is unfortunately impossible to say anything helpful about
those keyboard works (such as the Chromatic Fantasia) in
which series of block chords are marked *arpeggio*. They
come under the heading of free improvisation rather than
of ornamentation; and it appears that no models contemporary with J. S. Bach have been preserved. The player
will do well to base his interpretation on that of some
musicianly editor: to bear in mind Dolmetsch's method of
exhibiting part-writing (Ex. 221), and Emanuel Bach's
statement that the chords should be spread upwards and
downwards several times (Performance, §26): and not by
any means to consider himself bound to the printed notes
and the conventional arpeggio patterns.

Similar passages occur in string music. They are less
troublesome, because it is usually obvious that all the chords
are to be spread according to a given pattern (as in Ex. 222);

Ex. 222 Chaconne, bar 88. Autograph
arpeggio

and even when the pattern is not given (as in no. 65 of the St Matthew Passion), the player need do no more than invent a straightforward arpeggio figuration that suits his instrument.

The sign ⅃ sometimes occurs before a chord of only two notes (Ex. 223). In such cases an arpeggio would sound

Ex. 223   Three-part Invention in E flat, bar 21.   Autograph of 1723

feeble, and another explanation must be sought. It seems likely that Bach was harking back to the *Coulé sur vne tierce* of D'Anglebert or Dieupart (Ex. 224). This interpretation

Ex. 224   D'Anglebert

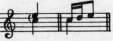

is supported, after a fashion, by ·Ex. 225; here it is obvious that the 'arpeggios' of bars 9–10 are parallel with the slides of bar 1. Note that throughout this version of the Invention —which is not authentic—these ornaments are best played before the beat.

Ex. 225   Three-part Invention in D minor.   Pseudo-autograph (P 219)
bar 1   from Landshoff

Another 'two-note arpeggio' occurs in Ex. 226. Again it

Ex. 226 French Overture, Ouverture, bar 6. OE

seems likely that Bach was harking back to D'Anglebert
(Ex. 227); the passage might be played in either of the ways
shown in Ex. 228.

THE ACCIACCATURA

THE present-day acciaccatura (♪) was not used by Bach. The sign occurs in modern editions, but is always wrong; it should be replaced by an ordinary small note. See p. 77.

The eighteenth-century textbooks are not very helpful; but one can see that the recommendations of Dolmetsch and Dannreuther are in accordance with the hints of Emanuel Bach, Marpurg, Türk, and Geminiani. The Bach acciaccatura was sometimes written as an ordinary note, sometimes as a sloping stroke. Ex. 229 illustrates an acciaccatura of the first type—the ♯*g* in the starred chord—and two interpretations.

Ex. 229   Partita III, Scherzo, bars 28–9.   OE

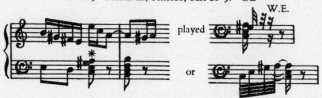

It seems that when this notation is used—it is common in Domenico Scarlatti, though this is the only example recorded in Bach—either interpretation is acceptable. If the chord is played *sec*, the acciaccatura must be released instantly (cf. the special mordent in Ex. 13). If the chord is spread, the acciaccatura is not held.

Emanuel Bach (Performance, §26) gives a specimen of the sloping-stroke sign (Ex. 230); this also is rather rare in his

Ex. 230   C.P.E.B.

father's music. It may stand alone (Ex. 231), or be combined with an arpeggio sign (Ex. 232); in either case, the chord is spread.

The notation of Exx. 231–2 is approximate; the accents show the positions of the beats.

Ex. 231   Partita VI, Sarabande, beginning.   OE★

Ex. 232   English Suite in A, Sarabande, beginning.   BG (Bischoff)

For other uses of the sloping-stroke sign—possibly not authentic—see Exx. 256–9.

★ The early autograph in Berlin MS P 225 has another acciaccatura between the *e* and *g* of the l.h.

THE commonest compound ornaments have already been discussed: the rising appoggiatura with mordent (Ex. 15) and the falling appoggiatura with a long or short shake (Exx. 110–13, 117, 156). For the combination of acciaccatura with arpeggio see Exx. 231–2.

The sign 𝄍 occurs once or twice. Emanuel Bach discusses it in his chapter on the Turn. He says it is like a short shake with closing-notes, and from the interpretations he gives in §§27 and 29 it appears that he would have played Ex. 233 somewhat as shown. In all his examples, the previous note is a step higher.

Ex. 233   Six Short Preludes, no. 1, bar 4.   BG

can be played

Based on C.P.E.B.

His father used this ornament in the rising context of Ex. 234. This was written about 1725. When the movement was engraved and published, in 1727 and again in 1731, the sign 𝄍 was replaced by an ambiguous scratch that might

Ex. 234   Partita III, Allemande, bar 6.   Autograph

mean anything from ∿ to ∿ ; see the reproduction, p. 150, no. 2. As a mordent is appropriate, and easier to play than any other ornament, no-one need hesitate to play one here. This, however, does not settle the question of what Bach meant by the sign 𝄍 in 1725.

Perhaps it is significant that J. G. Walther used this sign in both rising and falling contexts. In his music it can be played effectively either as a turn or as a shake with closing-notes.

When an appoggiatura is applied to one note of a chord, it is often effective to spread the chord, thus producing a combination of appoggiatura with arpeggio (cf. Ex. 231). Türk (p. 297) remarks that unless the appoggiatura is a very short one, the chord must be spread in such a way that the appoggiatura can make itself heard against the other notes of the chord. For this reason he prefers Ex. 235a to Marpurg's interpretation (b).

Ex. 235   Marpurg, 1755
  All[egro]   Türk   Tab. V, no. 23

As with plain arpeggios (Exx. 219–21), there seems no reason why players should not adopt downward interpretations, or more complicated ones, if they can see any advantage in doing so. In Ex. 236, the arpeggiation of the first chord is suggested by comparison with bar 145.

Ex. 236   French Overture, Ouverture, bars 1–2.   OE

played   or

Other combinations of ornaments occur, but most of them would be better described as close conjunctions. The two ornaments do not affect each other in any recognized way, but must first be interpreted separately, and then fitted together at the player's discretion.

The signs ✦ ∞ occur together in Ex. 237. They can be played in any of the three ways shown, and no doubt in several others that would be just as good (Marpurg, 1749, p. 65).

Ex. 237   Three-part Invention in E flat, bar 1.   Autograph of 1723

The signs ♒ ✦ occur in the pseudo-autograph of the inventions, whose ornamentation is almost certainly not authentic (Ex. 238). With the slide on the beat, they can be

Ex. 238   Three-part Invention in D minor, bar 17
Pseudo-autograph (P 219), from Landshoff

played as in Ex. 239a; but in this version of the movement

Ex. 239 a   b   W.E.

the slides probably come before the beat (see Ex. 225), in which case the interpretation will be as in b.

The combination ♪ *tr* occurs in an autograph oboe part of
Cantata 63, at bar 4 of the first duet (BG XVI. 76). It is an
alternative notation for ⟨ornament⟩, the latter being a keyboard sign
that an oboist might not have understood.

SUBSTITUTION

SUBSTITUTION is by no means a practice to be uncondi-
tionally recommended, for it is obviously undesirable that
a modern player should feel free to replace a well-authentic-
ated ornament by one that he finds easier to play. Anyone
who is inclined to do this should ask himself whether his
tempi are slow enough. Nevertheless, one often has to deal
with ornaments that are not well authenticated; and sometimes, try as one will, one cannot make a piece convincing
at the tempo necessitated by the ornaments Bach wrote. In
such cases it is better to play a simpler ornament than no
ornament at all.

Emanuel Bach shows how the ornamentation of a passage
can be simplified as the speed increases (Ex. 240; Embellishments, §19). The rough interpretations in Ex. 241 will serve
to show what he meant.

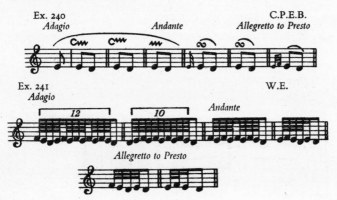

Four of these ornaments begin on the upper or lower auxiliaries; two on the main note. This is not a matter of opinion, but of fact: on this point, Emanuel's instructions are perfectly clear. It follows that the substitute need not begin on the same note as the original ornament.

There are probably only two types of substitution that are of any practical importance: that of an appoggiatura for a short shake, and that of a turn for a moderately long shake. Justification for both types will be found either in Ex. 240, or in Emanuel Bach (Trill, §18), or in Agricola (Ex. 276), or in J. S. Bach's own ornamentation. In Ex. 142 an appoggiatura is replaced by a short shake: in Ex. 37 a turn is used instead of a moderately long cadential shake.

ADDITION OF ORNAMENTS

THERE is no doubt that much of Bach's music is under-ornamented; but the addition of ornaments, in the full meaning of the words, is a matter that must be gone about even more cautiously than substitution, and only by experienced players who are thoroughly well acquainted with Bach's habits. Nevertheless, there is one type of addition that can and should be practised by everyone.

Figuration of the types shown in Ex. 242, most of which can be called cadential, always requires a shake of some kind at the point marked with a star; and it is important that the shake should be supplied.

These examples are types, not quotations.

Ex. 242

Whether the added shake should be long or short, and with or without closing-notes, depends on the tempo and the context; but it will always begin on the auxiliary. In such cases the auxiliary has a double function, melodic and harmonic; but whereas in *a* to *g* it is primarily a harmonic decoration—improving on the bald $\frac{5}{3}$ chord by suggesting a $\frac{5}{4}\frac{}{3}$ or $\frac{6}{4}\frac{5}{3}$— in *h* to *j* it is primarily melodic.

When a theme—or any recurrent piece of figuration—is ornamented at some of its entries, but not all, one has to think of ornamenting the rest. In Ex. 243, for instance, a mordent is presumably just as necessary in bar 12 as in bar 16.

Ex. 243   French Overture, Bourrée I.   OE

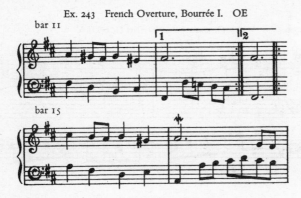

Again, if Bach ornamented the central cadence of a binary movement, it may be advisable to ornament the final cadence as well. In such cases, the ornamentation may have to be inverted. Compare Ex. 244 with Ex. 165; in Ex. 244 the additions to be made by the player are in square brackets.

Ex. 244   French Overture, Sarabande, end.   OE (emended)

Complete consistency is often impossible, for harmonic or other reasons; but it is sometimes clearly desirable.   An ornament may be one of the most noticeable features of a theme (Exx. 5, 27); and if the theme is played sometimes with and sometimes without its ornaments, listeners will find its entries difficult to recognize.   By adding ornaments systematically to a theme that Bach left unornamented, one can sometimes exhibit imitation in passages where it is easily overlooked.   Downes has given a practical demonstration of this by playing Ex. 245 as shown.

Ex. 245   Organ Fantasia in G minor, bars 31–5.   BG
Ornamentation by Carl Dolmetsch

In the accepted text of this passage there are no ornaments at all.

Aldrich has drawn an interesting distinction between ornaments (of any kind) that occur early in fugue subjects, and the cadential shakes with which they sometimes end. He thinks that the former (Exx. 5, 77) should, as far as possible, be played at every entry; but that with the latter, consistency is much less important. At the first two or three entries, and at other points where the texture is thin, the cadential shake may be valuable both as harmonic decoration and as a source of movement. When the texture is thicker, and provides its own movement and harmonic interest, the shake is less necessary. If Bach did not write it, the player is not bound to supply it.

In favour of strict consistency one can adduce E. L. Gerber's statement (Lexicon, 1790, col. 90) that Bach played the ornaments in his themes even when they occurred in the pedal part of an organ work, and Emanuel Bach's remark (Embellishments, §28) that all imitations must be exact to the smallest detail; but here and there one finds evidence suggesting that Bach's consistency was something less than absolute. However ingeniously one may solve the problem presented by Exx. 66–8, the fugue subject will not always begin in the same way; Bach himself made that impossible. Again, in the Finale of Organ Sonata IV, which is largely fugal, it is noteworthy that Bach ornamented all the manual entries, but neither of the pedal ones. And again, in the Organ Fugue in C the subject has a slide at only two of its entries (Ex. 28). As the slide comes early in the subject, it is covered by Aldrich's suggestion (referred to in the last paragraph); and one's first impulse might be to play a slide at every entry. As a matter of fact, the two authentic slides help to disguise hidden octaves between the extreme parts. There is only one other entry (the last) where this progression occurs, and it seems likely that that is the only point at which there is any need to add a slide.

Downes (*Musical Times*, Aug. 1947, p. 264) has drawn attention to a passage in which it may be said that Bach transferred a cadential shake from a fugue subject to another part (Ex. 246, bars 43–4).* Taking the hint, Downes proposes a similar transfer in bars 22–3. This is a most ingenious suggestion, which deserves to be borne in mind.

Ex. 246   Organ Fugue in F.   BG

bars 43–4   bars 22–3

MYSTERIES

THE following ornaments are probably a good deal less mysterious than the plain shake, if the truth were known; but they are rare in Bach, and have hardly been touched on by previous writers: moreover, some of them occur only in certain editions of pieces that are themselves practically

* Four similar transfers occur in the Finale of Organ Sonata IV, at bars 22, 24, 81, and 83.

unknown. There is therefore no consensus of opinion to fall
back on, and the following suggestions are tentative.

GROPPO

Ex. 247, recorded by Dannreuther, appears to be unique.

Ex. 247   Cantata 99, first movement, bars 35-7.   BG

Flute

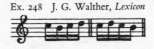

The *tr* and *groppo* are in the autograph full score, but not
in the original flute part.

The passage recurs later in the movement, at the end of
the sixth line of the chorale. Here it is transposed into D
and given to the oboe d'amore; there is a *tr*, but no *groppo*.

Another version of this movement occurs in Cantata 100
(first chorus). Here, both passages have simply *tr*.

To J. G. Walther the term *groppo* seems to have meant
not an ornament, but a type of written-out decorative
figuration (comparable with *Nota Cambiata*). He speaks of
a *groppo ascendente* and a *groppo descendente* (Ex. 248), and

Ex. 248   J. G. Walther, *Lexicon*

says that this figuration is often used at the end of a shake.

To Marpurg the term had much the same meaning in
1749 (p. 83); but in 1756 he applied it to a kind of turn
(Ex. 249).

Ex. 249   Marpurg, 1756, Tab. VI
no. 8   no. 7   Effect

Dannreuther was probably right in suggesting that Bach
meant nothing more recondite than closing-notes (Ex. 250).

H

Ex. 250   W.E.

As the *groppo* is neither in Cantata 100 nor in the oboe d'amore passage of Cantata 99, and even in bar 36 occurs only in the score—not in the flute part, which was the important thing to get right—it seems most unlikely that Bach wanted anything really unusual.

SMALL NOTES

One sometimes comes across small notes that are neither appoggiaturas nor Nachschlags. Those starred in Ex. 251 (and others in the same movement) appear to be authentic. Presumably they should be played quickly and before the beat, just as they are written—like modern grace-notes.

Ex. 251   Three-part Invention in E flat.   Autograph of 1723

There is no extant autograph of Ex. 252, and these ornaments may not be authentic. Those in bars 10 and 13 are
almost certainly wrong.

Ex. 252   Organ Trio in D minor.   Peters

bar 1   bar 13   bar 4

bar 10

Bar 13 should presumably agree with bar 1. Both might
then be played as in Ex. 253. The same rhythmical pattern
will serve in bar 4.

Ex. 253
bar 1   W.E.

In bar 10 the small notes should probably be *e''* and *d''*,
not *f''* and *e''*. Thus emended, they make a written-out
mordent. Some manuscripts have a mordent here (Ex. 254);
and this is the safest interpretation.

Ex. 254
bar 10   BG

SLOPING STROKES

The sloping strokes in Exx. 231–2 mean arpeggios with
acciaccaturas; and a somewhat similar interpretation may
serve in Ex. 255. Dannreuther's interpretation, based on a
lutenist's sign that was adopted by Pachelbel, seems rather
dull.

Ex. 255 Aria Variata. BG

bar 5

possibly   W.E.

Dannreuther

The sloping stroke in bar 4 of Ex. 256 is not authentic. It seems likely that the person who wrote it, whoever he was,

Ex. 256 Three-part Invention in E minor, bars 1–4
Pseudo-autograph (P 219), from Landshoff

had in mind a slide or a *tierce coulée*; but if so, he misplaced the sign. The correct interpretation (Ex. 257) can be deduced from bar 2.

Ex. 257   W.E.
bar 4

If the autograph of *c.* 1725, quoted in Ex. 258a, were the

only text of this Sarabande, one would probably read the
sloping stroke as a *tierce coulée*, by analogy with Couperin
(1713), Gottlieb Muffat, and other authors. The situation is
complicated by the editions of 1727 and 1731, in both of

Ex. 258   Partita III, Sarabande, bars 7–8
Autograph   *Tierce coulée*   OE

which the passage appears somewhat as in *c*. It is obvious
that the engraver made a mistake, and it is natural to suppose
that the *c″* and *e″* were meant to be semiquavers. The passage
has indeed been thus corrected (in manuscript) by early
owners of the British Museum copy of the 1727 edition and
the Hirsch copy of 1731; and in any case there is nothing in
the editions to suggest that a *d″* ought to be played, as in a
tierce coulée.

Bach may have changed his mind about the figuration
here, and replaced the ornament (whatever it was) by the
two semiquavers. On the other hand, the semiquavers may
be an actual interpretation of the stroke—Bach may always
have meant the passage to be played as it appears in the
editions, and have changed his notation simply because he
found that the stroke was likely to be misunderstood. Its
meaning remains uncertain; but in the present state of our
knowledge it is difficult to justify a *tierce coulée* here.

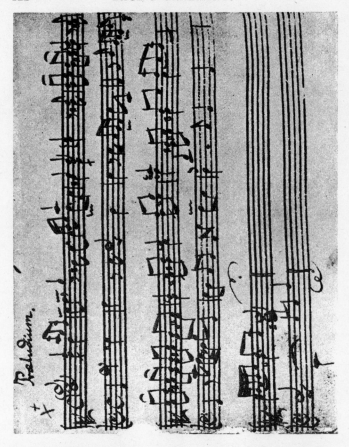

The little piece reproduced above, and transcribed opposite, has been printed among Bach's works in BG XXXVI. 237. As a matter of fact, the writing may not be Bach's, and the composer was most probably French. The ornamentation is nevertheless of some interest, since it must have been familiar in the Bach household, and may throw light on other passages.

Ex. 259   Praeludium   From the **W. F. Bach** *Clavierbüchlein*

a. Bars 1–2. These comma-like signs are presumably mordents (D'Anglebert, Dieupart, Rameau).

b. Bars 1, 3, 6. These sloping strokes—through the stem, not
between note-heads as in Ex. 256—mean arpeggios,
according to D'Anglebert and Dieupart. In bars 1 and 6
one might try the *tierce coulée* (Ex. 224); the chord in
bar 3 might be spread, with or without acciaccaturas.

c. Bar 2. See Ex. 116.

d. Bars 3, 4. See Exx. 223-4.

e. Bars 6, 7. All four hooks seem to be too high; these must
surely be rising appoggiaturas.

SHORT SHAKES

FOUR kinds of short shake are described by various eighteenth-century authors. They are set forth in Exx. 260–3, with the names that will be used in the following discussion.

Ex. 260 Trillo   Explication

Ex. 261 Pralltriller
C.P.E.B., Trill, §30   Agricola, p. 103

Ex. 262 Schneller   Türk, p. 251

Ex. 263 Imperfect Shake   Marpurg, 1755 (Tab. V, no. 1)

Marpurg gives two reasons for calling the shakes in Ex. 263 imperfect: they consist of three notes only, and they begin on the main note. In the second of these senses, the following shakes from the Explication are imperfect: the actual shakes begin on the main note (Ex. 264).

Ex. 264   Explication

In arguing from the Explication, as from other tables that are evidently concerned with general principles, it is permissible, and indeed necessary, to take certain liberties. It is not to be supposed that Bach's Trillos always consisted of exactly six notes: or that ornaments like those in Ex. 264 always consisted of appoggiaturas followed by exactly five notes, and were always indicated by *long* shake-signs. When such allowances have been made, the Explication can be said to authorize two interpretations of the sign ∾. Combined with an appoggiatura—or preceded by the note a step higher, which comes to much the same thing (Ex. 278*e*, *f*)—it is an Imperfect Shake of five notes (reducible, of course, to three at discretion). Otherwise it is a Trillo of six notes (reducible to four).

The question arises whether Bach ever used Pralltrillers and Schnellers. Admittedly, the Explication does not mention them; but then, neither does it mention the Arpeggio, Acciaccatura, and Slide. Thus, although the Explication does not authorize the Pralltriller and Schneller, it cannot reasonably be said to forbid them.

Evidence for the Pralltriller

Under various names and with various signs, the Pralltriller was undoubtedly in use during Bach's lifetime. Ex. 62 shows Muffat's version of it (*c.* 1730). The second ornament in Ex. 86 (Marpurg, 1755) is a slightly lengthened Pralltriller; and the whole of Ex. 86 seems to have been borrowed from Couperin (1713). Emanuel Bach and Agricola both mention the Pralltriller; and they had both been pupils of J. S. Bach's. On the whole, it seems likely that he used it occasionally; and from certain passages in his music, as also from Emanuel and Agricola, one can guess at suitable contexts.

Obviously, a Pralltriller can only be used if the note before the shake is a step higher; and most probably this previous note ought also to be accented. The passage must be legato, and the ornament is, on the whole, most likely to occur in slow expressive pieces. Furthermore, despite Emanuel Bach and Türk, a Pralltriller cannot reasonably be used unless there is movement in another part at the beginning of the shake (see Exx. 144–9). If there is no movement, it is better to use an Imperfect Shake.

From Agricola one gathers that a short shake should always be played as a Pralltriller when it is preceded by an appoggiatura that is written as a small note or hook. In Bach, passages of this type that satisfy the above conditions seem to be extremely rare; it usually happens that there is no movement in the other parts (Ex. 156). The shake in Ex. 171 could be a Pralltriller; but it may not be authentic. The shake in Ex. 164, which has been interpreted as a Pralltriller in Ex. 165, is authentic; but the appoggiaturas in the second-time bar, however obvious it may seem that Bach meant them, are not in the original edition.

According to Marpurg (and Türk, p. 273), when the note before a shake is a step higher, and the two notes are slurred, the slur can be treated as a tie. In other words, if the shake has to be played short, it is a Pralltriller. See Ex. 86 (Couperin–Marpurg), the unusual sign used by Muffat in Ex. 62, and Emanuel Bach's notation in Ex. 261.

Passages of the types shown in Ex. 265 are not uncommon in J. S. Bach, and in both cases a Pralltriller is effective.

Ex. 265   XVIII, no. 9, *Nun komm*.   Autograph

bar 16

can be played

W.E.

Bar 7 of this same prelude (Ex. 266) is parallel with bar 31. There is an early version of this movement, from which

Ex. 266 The same

it can be deduced that there ought to be a slur in bar 7; and in any case it is obvious that the ornament should be played like that in bar 31. As omission of slurs is a common error, a Pralltriller is sometimes justifiable in unslurred passages like Ex. 267.

Ex. 267 Orgelbüchlein, *Wenn wir*, bar 3. Autograph

The Pralltriller is never necessary in J. S. Bach, and must
be used with discretion. The 'safe' interpretation is the Imperfect Shake authorized by the Explication; it is only because
the Explication is not altogether satisfactory as evidence that
the Pralltriller has to be considered at all.

The Schneller: Description and Use

The Schneller may have been known to Couperin (1717,
p. 23) as a form of 'arbitrary shake';* but it was not properly
described by anyone connected with the Bach circle until
three years after Bach's death. Nevertheless, if one reads
the post-Bach textbooks carefully—remembering that, as
with all ancient authors, what they actually say may be
much less important than what they imply, or do not even
hint at—one finds reason to believe that the Schneller was
established in the Bach circle before 1753, and that the reason
why it had not been described before was simply that it had
been confused with the other forms of short shake, and
indicated by the same sign (⬩⬩). There may have been, as
there still is, a tendency to use the Schneller to excess; and
perhaps it was to combat this tendency that Emanuel Bach
gave the ornament a name and a sign of its own.

His account of the Schneller is quoted and translated in
Appendix II. It will be observed that he refers to it quite
casually as 'the inverted short mordent'; his tone is that of
a man who is giving an easily recognizable description of
a well-known ornament, and he does not trouble to
give an interpretation. He does not say that the Schneller
is new, or even of recent origin: only that no-one else had
described it. He says his notation is invariable; this means
that some other notation had been in use, and still was.

* He seems to have been in the habit of prolonging the first and last notes
of his shakes. The prolonged first note, which amounted to an appoggiatura
opening, he called the *appuy*: the last note, the *point d'arrest*. Other kinds of
shake, he says, are arbitrary; some of them are so short that they have neither
appuy nor *point d'arrest*, and one can even play shakes staccato (*On en peut
faire même d'aspirés*. In his table of 1713, an *Aspiration* is a staccato dash).
The description is suggestive, but miserably vague; it is most unfortunate
that he did not give musical illustrations.

Further, his ideas about the Schneller are far from clear, even in 1787—thirty-four years after he first described it. First, he says it is an inverted short mordent, opposed to the mordent both in shape and in use: then, that its notes are absolutely the same as those of the Pralltriller (this is manifestly untrue, although one can see what he means): next, that it sounds very much like a plain shake: and elsewhere (in his discussion of the mordent, §14) it is the Pralltriller, not the Schneller, that he opposes to the mordent, the two ornaments being used respectively in descending and ascending contexts.

This description tells one more about the state of Emanuel's mind than about the Schneller. The distinction between it and the Pralltriller may possibly have been clear in his playing; but he was unable to explain it in words, either because he lacked literary skill, or because he had not reasoned it out properly.

From this pioneer description of the Schneller it is convenient to pass on to Türk's—the last that need be quoted. It is fairly consistent with Emanuel's, but clearer and more detailed. Türk gives an interpretation (Ex. 262), and the following examples showing the use of the ornament (Ex. 268). His commentary may be summarized thus: the

Ex. 268   Türk, p. 252

Schneller is used when a note is repeated [weak to strong], as in *a*: especially in descending passages (*b*): [on the accented notes] in a descending scale (*c*): at a half-cadence (*d*): after a rest (*e*): before a leap (*f*): and on the second of *two* notes rising by step (*g*). It must never be used on passing-notes (*h*).

Marpurg gives some examples that resemble Türk's *f* and *g*, and also an unaccented one (Ex. 269).

Ex. 269   Marpurg, 1755–6 (Tab. V, no. 6)

This clears up the interpretation and use of the Schneller. It is an inverted mordent in the strict sense of the term. Like the mordent, it is primarily an accent; but being an inversion of the mordent, it can be used in passages that move in the opposite direction to those that suit the mordent. It thus seems likely that when Emanuel Bach opposed the mordent to the Pralltriller (Mordent, §14) he was confusing the Pralltriller with the Schneller.

The Schneller: Confusion with the Pralltriller and Trillo

Türk provides further evidence of the confusion that reigned between about 1750 and 1789. In his discussion of the Pralltriller, he insists that the only correct interpretation is the tied one. Some authors, he admits (Marpurg is one, although Türk does not name him) have interpreted ⁓ as an Imperfect Shake; but this notation, though more convenient, is wrong.

Türk goes on to say that the Pralltriller ought to occur only on the second note of a falling second, and that it does not matter whether the first note is written as a large note or as an appoggiatura. (In this he differs from Agricola, who says that after a large note the sign ⁓ is played as a Trillo.) Nevertheless, he says, even the best composers have made some exceptions to this rule; and he quotes (Ex. 270) from

the works of [Emanuel] Bach, E. W. Wolf, and others
whom he does not name. In all these examples, he says, the
Pralltriller has been confused with the Schneller, and the
latter would have been right. He concludes, 'I leave it to the
critics to decide how great a crime this may be.'

Ex. 270   Türk, p. 273

It will be observed that Türk himself has confused the
Pralltriller with the Trillo. The ornaments in Ex. 270 may
be Trillos or Schnellers; but they cannot possibly be Pralltrillers.

To understand the passage one must realize that Türk
was trying hard to be systematic—so hard that he over-
reached himself. He had a genuine complaint: the ambiguity
of the sign ⌇. In his opinion—and he was probably right—
the composers quoted in Ex. 270 wanted Schnellers. They
ought therefore to have used Emanuel Bach's notation (two
small notes); had all composers done so, the sign ⌇ could
have been confined to the Pralltriller and the Trillo. (It will
be remembered that Türk did not recognize the Imperfect
Shake.) This was evidently Türk's object, and it was a
sensible one; but in attacking one form of confusion he fell
into another himself, and failed to distinguish between the
Pralltriller and the Trillo.

The same confusion is apparent in his footnote, to the
effect that if a composer wants a Pralltriller in passages like
Ex. 270b, he had better insert an appoggiatura, as in Ex. 271.

Ex. 271   Türk, p. 273

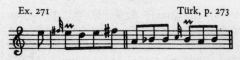

The ornaments in Ex. 271 cannot be played as Pralltrillers; the object of the appoggiatura is to make players interpret the sign ⁗ as a Trillo, not as a Schneller.

Thus, in 1789 the sign ⁗ was likely to be interpreted as a Schneller; in fact, it *meant* a Schneller, as well as a Trillo or Pralltriller. It was probably ambiguous as early as 1760, for the small note in Ex. 272 appears to be a precautionary

Ex. 272   C. P. E. Bach, Six Sonatas with varied Reprises, p. 1.   1760

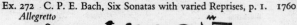

appoggiatura like those in Ex. 271. The date can be pushed back still further. Emanuel's emphasis on his invariable notation clearly implies that some other notation of the Schneller was in use in and before 1753; and if this other notation was not the sign ⁗, what was it?

In this way one can account not only for Emanuel's attitude, but also for most of the other confusions and contradictions in the textbooks of 1753–89.

At first sight, this may seem to be inconsistent with Türk's remark (p. 251, §24): 'As it has no sign of its own (in Ermangelung eines eigenen Zeichens), it is indicated by two small notes'; but this is not so. 'As it has no sign of its own' need not—and indeed cannot—mean that the Schneller had never had any sign at all until Emanuel Bach gave it one in 1753; it means that the Schneller had formerly shared a sign (⁗) with other ornaments—the other forms of short shake.

Emanuel Bach's own notation of the Schneller may not have been as invariable as he said it was; when he wrote

those emphatic words, he may have been thinking only of
the Sonatas that he published as musical illustrations to the
Versuch. Ex. 273 was published seven years later. According

Ex. 273   C. P. E. Bach, Six Sonatas with varied Reprises, p. 17.   1760

to Emanuel the sign ᷉ means a Pralltriller, and nothing
else—not even a Trillo—; but in the third whole bar of this
passage it is inconceivable that he played a Pralltriller. He
may have meant a Trillo; but a Schneller seems not at all
unlikely.

It must be remembered that Emanuel was, according to
Türk, one of the composers who misused the sign ᷉ in
Ex. 270.

Confusion due to the Imperfect Shake

The Schneller and the Pralltriller have very little in common. They both use the upper auxiliary; but whereas the
former usually occurs on strongly accented staccato notes,
the latter—being a decorated resolution of an appoggiatura—
is always slurred to the previous note, and always unaccented.

Had there been no other forms of short shake, it is charit-
able to suppose that even eighteenth-century authors and
composers would have seen the difference, and found a
separate sign for the Schneller, long before 1753; but the
situation was complicated by the Trillo, and, much more
seriously, by the Imperfect Shake. Except that it is not tied,
the Trillo is identical with the Pralltriller in its notes; but,
like the Schneller, it can be used as an accent. The Imperfect
Shake resembles the Pralltriller in that it occurs in legato
passages and is often unaccented; but in its notes it is identical
with the Schneller, and it sometimes carries at any rate a
weak accent. The following examples will show how

difficult it must have been to distinguish between the Pralltriller, Schneller, and Imperfect Shake.

On quick notes, according to Emanuel Bach, the Pralltriller must be played so fast that the listener will not notice that the ornamented note has been shortened [i.e., delayed by the tie]; he should feel that it has been played at the right moment. Applying these instructions to one of the examples in the *Versuch*, one arrives at the interpretation of Ex. 274—

Ex. 274   C.P.E.B.   W.E.

which gives point to Emanuel's remark (§32) that the Pralltriller must not sound as terrifying as it would look if it were written out. Except in a very slow tempo, it would have been practically indistinguishable from the Imperfect Shake in Ex. 275; and since in this example the *e'* is more

Ex. 275   W.E.

strongly accented than the *d'* that follows it, this Imperfect Shake is indistinguishable from a Schneller except by the fact that it is slurred.

One cannot help suspecting—especially after reading Marpurg's remarks, quoted below—that Emanuel Bach's elaborate explanation serves chiefly to disguise the fact that in Ex. 274 he played not Pralltrillers but Imperfect Shakes. He may well have felt that if once he allowed himself to give the sign ∿ more than one meaning, the intricacies of its interpretation would be too much for him.

The post-Bach Tradition

On the whole, it seems likely that by 1750, and perhaps a good deal earlier, the sign ∿ had three or four meanings for

members of the Bach circle. The various interpretations, and
their proper contexts, would have been just as difficult to
distinguish then as they are now. It would hardly be an
exaggeration to say that only the composer knew what he
meant by the sign; and he himself may have changed his
mind from time to time.

As authors of textbooks, Emanuel Bach and his successors
were thus confronted with an exceptionally difficult problem;
and it is not surprising that they failed to solve it completely.
In their attempts to write systematically they seem—naturally
enough—to have neglected subtle distinctions observed by
performers to whom they looked for guidance, and even
distinctions that they themselves observed instinctively. This
failing is not uncommon among musicians today, and is
indeed very difficult to avoid. Thus, although the textbooks
of 1753–89 seem at first sight to reflect two distinct traditions,
each fairly clear but inconsistent with the other, it may be
that in fact they reflect different aspects of a single tradition,
which was consistent in actual practice, but so full of subtleties
as to be almost indescribable.

The figuration of Ex. 274 is of a type that was generally
considered suitable for the sign ⁕; and this example naturally
appears, without essential modification, in the writings of
Agricola, Marpurg, J. C. F. Bach, and Türk. It is instructive
to compare their remarks and interpretations.

Emanuel Bach's point of view has already been presented
in Ex. 274.

Agricola does not give a written-out interpretation; but it
appears that he would have played the passage as in Ex. 276.

Ex. 276   W.E., based on Agricola, pp. 99, 104, 111
in fast tempi

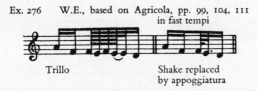

Trillo   Shake replaced
                          by appoggiatura

Türk also does not give a written-out interpretation; but
no doubt he would have agreed with Emanuel Bach.

These three authors, if taken literally, represent one tradition—according to which short shakes indicated by the sign ⌁ ought always. to begin with the auxiliary, tied or untied.

The other tradition—according to which short shakes indicated by ⌁ sometimes begin with the main note—is represented by J. C. F. Bach and Marpurg. The former gives a written-out interpretation, which is transcribed, with all its mistakes, in Ex. 277.

Ex. 277   J. C. F. Bach (1787)

Marpurg gives the written-out interpretations of Ex. 278.

Ex. 278   Marpurg, 1755-6 (Tab. V, nos 1-4)

The exact position of the slurs is uncertain.

Examples *a*, *b*, and *c* are meant to go fairly fast (*bey geschwinder Bewegung, un peu vif.*)

Marpurg expressly says that *f* is simply another way of writing *e*. This shows that a slurred large note may call for the same interpretation as an appoggiatura, and helps to justify the treatment of slurs as ties in Exx. 114–5, 148. See also Exx. 42 and 86, and Agricola's remarks referred to on p. 126.

Ex. *h* is in essentials the same as one of Emanuel Bach's (Trill, §34). Emanuel does not give an interpretation; but if he is to be taken at his word, he would have played Pralltrillers throughout Ex. 278.

An alternative notation of *g* has been omitted.

It may be thought that Exx. 277–8 illustrate the error remarked on by Türk (p. 130, above)—that the notation used by certain authors was chosen for its convenience, and did not represent their intentions accurately. This may or may not be true of J. C. F. Bach; but it is certainly not true of Marpurg, whose discussion shows that he preferred Imperfect Shakes, played them himself, and thought Emanuel Bach played them also. After speaking of those contexts where the previous note is a step higher than the ornamented note, he continues (1755, p. 56):

If one passes over the tied note of a simple Tied Shake [Ex. 86*b*], begins at once on the main note (contrary to the rule for shakes), and cuts the repercussions down to three notes, the result is a shake that, though admittedly imperfect [*unvollkommner*], sounds better than the ordinary perfect shake in certain cases. These cases are:

in fast passages descending by step [Ex. 278*a, b, c*]
when a short note is preceded by a long appoggiatura [Ex. 278*d*]
when a [long] note is shortened by an appoggiatura [Ex. 278*e, f*].

Except in the notation, there is no difference between *e* and *f*.

On account of the speed [*Schnelligkeit*] with which one must play these three notes (and not more than three), Herr [Emanuel] Bach calls this shake a Pralltriller. He remarks further that when it occurs on a pause, one makes the appoggiatura very long, and then snaps off smartly with this shake, lifting the finger off the key quickly [Ex. 278 *g, h*].

If one wishes to introduce a Pralltriller suddenly on a note [*plötzlich auf einer Note*. Marpurg means, when the previous note is not a step higher] one must either write it out just as it is to be played, or write two small notes—those with which the repercussions are made—just before the main note. [Here he gives Ex. 269, and also two examples that resemble Ex. 268*f* and *g*.] Herr [Emanuel] Bach calls this ornament a Schneller. It is simply an Inverted Short Mordent, both in this case, when it is written out in notes, and in the previous case, when it is an abbreviated shake following an appoggiatura, and is called a Pralltriller. Chapter VII, which deals with the Mordent, will make this clear. Nevertheless, one must never call a Schneller a Mordent, as is the ridiculous habit of certain clavier-players. One must always call ornaments by their proper names.

Badly as Marpurg expressed himself, one can see that he had a clearer head than either Emanuel Bach or Türk; the passage quoted above can be accepted as a fairly precise account of his own practice. It is remarkable not only for its comparative precision, but also for its comprehensiveness. Marpurg has been cited here as representing the 'main-note tradition'; but this is not the whole truth, for he represented the other tradition as well. He recognized the Trillo, in the prolonged form authorized by the Explication (Ex. 86*a*): the Pralltriller, in the prolonged form of Ex. 86*b*: the Imperfect Shake, in a shorter form than that of the Explication: and finally the Schneller. Here as elsewhere, prolongation and abbreviation are matters of convenience and personal taste.* It is therefore fair to say that, of all the authors quoted, Marpurg was the only one who recognized all four forms of the short shake, and made an honest attempt to deal with them; and his opinions deserve more respect than those of Emanuel Bach, who ignored two forms, or those of Türk, who refused to recognize one of the forms and confused two of the others.

The two forms that Emanuel Bach ignored are precisely those that his father recognized. If the Explication means anything at all, Sebastian Bach would have agreed with Marpurg in Ex. 278*d*, *e*, *g*, and *h*. They would both have played Imperfect Shakes, whereas Emanuel would have played Pralltrillers—or so he leaves one to suppose. The possibility that Bach would have played Imperfect Shakes

---

* Except so far as Marpurg's Imperfect Shake consisted of three notes 'and not more than three', a rule that is to be regarded as valid for his own performances and compositions.

in Ex. 278*a*, *b*, and *c*—not uncommon types of context—
can therefore not be excluded.

Conclusion

Thanks to the inadequacy of the Explication, and the
contradictory statements of Bach's successors, the truth about
his treatment of the sign ⁓ has remained obscure for some
two hundred years; and much of it must now be regarded
as beyond recovery. In any case, it will not be recovered by
taking the Explication literally, as if it were an all-sufficient
guide: or by minimizing the differences between the various
authors in an attempt to reconcile them. It will be more
profitable to try to find out whether the differences are
genuine, or due to careless or unskilful literary work; and
further, to try to explain how it was that the post-Bach
authors found it so extraordinarily difficult to say what they
meant.

My own explanation is that the four forms of Short Shake
were all in use in the Bach circle: that although there was
a vague differentiation between the various forms, they
were frequently indistinguishable to the listener: that they
accordingly became confused: and that the confusion was
made worse by the post-Bach authors, who, in their
attempts to be systematic, tended either to disregard some
of the forms or to describe more than one of them under a
single name.

No doubt this explanation is incomplete; but it does at least
allow one to vary the treatment of the sign ⁓ according to
the context. The results are illustrated systematically in
Exx. 138–56; but for convenience, some further examples are
appended.

As the four short shakes in Ex. 279 are not strongly
accented, they cannot be Schnellers; and Trillos would break
the legato. If these objections are valid, there remain two
possible interpretations: Pralltrillers and Imperfect Shakes.

Ex. 279   Italian Concerto ii.   OE

At *a* and *d*, Pralltrillers have the advantage that they add
harmonic interest by introducing suspensions.   At *c* an
Imperfect Shake will help to preserve the appoggiatura-
effect of the note *a'*.   The treatment of *b* is very much a
matter of personal opinion.

On the other hand, in Ex. 280 Pralltrillers and Imperfect
Shakes are out of the question; the ornaments must be Trillos
or Schnellers.   Emanuel Bach and Türk both say that

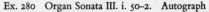

Ex. 280   Organ Sonata III. i. 50–2.   Autograph

Schnellers are appropriate at half-cadences (Exx. 268*d*, 282);
and it seems possible that Sebastian Bach would have agreed
with them.   At any rate, it is doubtful whether there is
anything to be gained by playing Trillos.

Finally, in Ex. 10 the signs ∿ and ⩘ are directly opposed:
the former in descending, the latter in ascending contexts.

No-one seems to doubt that the mordents ought to be played, as it were, *c b c*. Is it reasonable that they should be answered by inexact inversions reading *d c d c*?

APPENDIX II

EMANUEL BACH ON THE SCHNELLER

TEXT: *Versuch*, 1787, p. 83. The passage marked †† is not in the first edition (1753).

1. Den kurzen Mordent in der Gegen-Bewegung, dessen höchsten Ton man schnellt, und die übrigen beyden mit dem steifen Finger vorträget, habe ich jederzeit, ohne Veränderung, so angedeutet, wie wir Tab. VI unter Fig. XCIV [Ex. 281] sehen. Wegen dieses Schnellens kann man diese noch sonsten nicht bemerkte Manier gar wohl den S c h n e l l e r

Ex. 281

nennen. †Diese Manier ist so wohl in der Bewegung der Noten, als im Gebrauche das Gegentheil vom Mordenten. In den Noten ist sie dem Prall-Triller vollkommen ähnlich.†

2. Dieser Schneller wird allezeit geschwinde gemacht und kommt niemals anders als bey gestossenen und geschwinden Noten vor, welchen er einen Glanz giebt, und wo er just zur Ausfüllung zureicht.

3. Er thut in der Geschwindigkeit die Würkung eines Trillers ohne Nachschlag, und gleichwie der letztere mit dem Nachschlage eine steigende Folge liebt, so mag der Schneller gerne herunter gehende Noten nach sich haben, ohne Zweifel, weil sein letztes kleines Nötgen und die Haupt-Note zusammen genommen einen Nachschlag von dem Triller in der Gegen-Bewegung vorstellen. Dem ohngeachtet unterscheidet er sich von den Trillern dadurch, dass er niemals angeschlossen und bey Schleifungen vorkommen kann.

4. Er muss sehr geschickt ausgeübt werden, weil er sich
sonst nicht gut ausnimmt. Es können ihn daher blos die
stärkesten und fertigsten Fingen [sic] bewerkstelligen, und
man muss aus Noth oft mit einem Finger fortgehen, welches
dem Stossen, so ihm natürlich ist, keinen Schaden thut,
Fig. XCV (a) [Ex. 282a]. Man kann diese Manier besonders
auch bey den Einschnitten brauchen (b).

Ex. 282

TRANSLATION: cf. Mitchell, p. 142.   The passage marked
†† is not in the first edition (1753).

1. For the Inverted Short Mordent I have always, without
variation, used the notation of Ex. 281. Its upper note is
snapped; the other two are played with a stiff finger. On
account of the snap (Wegen dieses Schnellens), this ornament,
not noticed elsewhere, may well be called the Schneller. †In
its shape and use it is the opposite of the Mordent. In its notes
it is absolutely the same as the Pralltriller. †

2. The Schneller is always played fast, and occurs only on
quick notes that are accented and detached (gestossen). It
gives such notes brilliance, and just suffices to fill them out.

3. It is gone in a moment, leaving the effect of a shake
without closing-notes. Just as a shake *with* closing-notes is
best suited to a rising step, so the Schneller is best when
followed by a descent. No doubt this is because the last of
its small notes, together with its main note, forms an inversion of the closing-notes of a shake. Nevertheless it differs
from shakes, in that it never follows an appoggiatura and is
never slurred.

4. It does not sound well unless it is played pat. Only the
strongest and best fingers can bring it off, and for this reason
one must often continue with a single finger. This does no

harm, since staccato contexts are proper to the Schneller
(Ex. 282a).* It is particularly appropriate at half-cadences (b).

POSTSCRIPT

THE following material came to my attention too late to be
incorporated in the body of this book.

J. D. HEINICHEN, Der General-Bass in der Composition,
Dresden, 1728.

Heinichen (1683–1729) studied under Kuhnau about 1700,
spent the years 1710–16 in Italy, and became Capellmeister
at Dresden in 1717. At the Dresden Opera he worked with
A. Lotti until 1720, when the company was disbanded. He
cannot be regarded as a safe guide to the interpretation of
Bach's ornaments; indeed, the main interest of his views
lies in the fact that some of them are startlingly different from
those that are supposed to have been held in the Bach circle.
This supports my statement (p. 9) that the purchasers of
Bach's published works would have played his ornaments
in all kinds of different ways.

It must be understood that Heinichen does not deal
systematically with ornaments. He is concerned with
ornamentation in a wider sense—the elaboration of a continuo part. Such ornamentation, he says, is of two kinds:
firstly, the addition of a melodic upper part, or the use of
arpeggios and passage-work: secondly, the employment of
'those little ornaments that always remain the same, just as
you learnt them from your teacher'. The ornaments discussed below are of this latter kind.

Ex. 283 gives Heinichen's notation for an appoggiatura
and a slide. Exx. 284–5 show how he would have them
sung and played.

* The German is obscure, but this must be what Emanuel meant. Türk
(p. 251) remarks that as the Schneller occurs only on short staccato notes,
one can take liberties with the fingering.

Ex. 283   Heinichen, p. 527

Ex. 284   As sung   p. 528

Ex. 285   As played   p. 528

He then gives examples, in some of which the interpretations of Ex. 285 cannot be applied.

His interpretations of the slide are interesting for two
reasons. Firstly, it is just possible—though anyone who is
acquainted with eighteenth-century textbooks will realize
that it is extremely unlikely—that when he wrote of 'those
little ornaments that always remain . . . just as you learnt
them from your teacher', he meant exactly what he said.
On this very dangerous assumption, the interpretations in
Exx. 284–5 might perhaps be based on Kuhnau's practice,
and might thus throw light on Exx. 20–1.

Secondly, interpretations of the type shown in Ex. 284
(or even Ex. 285) can be applied to Ex. 28. I have already
remarked (p. 27) that these slides cannot be played before
the beat, in the Waltherian manner, for then they make
octaves. I have also remarked (p. 116) that if they are played
in the orthodox way, *on* the beat, they help to disguise
hidden octaves between extreme parts. For this purpose
Heinichen's interpretations are even more effective (Ex. 286).

Ex. 286   Organ Fugue in C
bar 18   W.E.

From the amount of space that Heinichen devotes to the subject, it is evident that mordents were often played with wrong auxiliary notes even in 1728. Only one of his examples adds anything to what I have already said.

He does not give a written-out interpretation of the mordent; but his verbal descriptions of three possible interpretations can be represented somewhat as in Ex. 287 (cf. F. T.

Ex. 287   based on Heinichen, p. 530

Arnold, *Thorough-Bass*, p. 451). The first and second are to be played with extreme rapidity; the third is used by 'some players' on 'slow notes'. It is probable that to Heinichen the term *mordent* usually meant the ornament that in this book is called *acciaccatura*. In studying Ex. 288, this must be borne in mind.

Ex. 288   Heinichen, p. 533

The mordents are indicated by the sign // (cf. Exx. 20–1); and the only ones that are at all remarkable have been numbered.

Mordent (2) is expressly sharpened, as one would expect.

Mordent (1) also is expressly sharpened; and this means that in Heinichen's opinion the key is already E minor.

Mordent (3) is presumably to be played with ♯*c*.

ALFRED KREUTZ: Urtext edition of Bach's English Suites, 1950 (Peters, no. 4580 *a*, *b*), with an eight-page essay, *Die Ornamentik in J. S. Bachs Klavierwerken*. English translation in Hinrichsen's *Music Book*, VII (1952).

Consideration of the general history of ornaments has led Kreutz to conclusions not unlike some of those put forward in this book:

That slides are not always played *on* the beat:

That shakes do not always begin on the auxiliary note:

That closing-notes are not always as fast as the shake itself:

That closing-notes do not always follow the pattern laid down in the Explication:

That single small notes (usually read as appoggiaturas) are often played *before* the beat as in Ex. 158.

His recommendations are, as a rule, musically satisfying; and if it is sometimes difficult to detect their historical bases, that may be only because he had too little space to develop his arguments fully.

Two other results of his are of great importance, and call for discussion here. The first concerns a special type of Long Mordent; the second concerns the Schneller.

The Gigue of the English Suite in D minor is in the usual binary form, with the thematic material largely inverted in the second half. In the first half there are a number of shakes: in the second half, a number of ornaments that have always been printed as shakes, but are in fact full-length mordents (Couperin's *pincé continu*).

There is no autograph of the English Suites; but this reading is satisfactorily established. In the second half of this Gigue, the notation is ✢ or ✦✇, according to the space available; sometimes ∿✦, owing to misplacement of the vertical stroke. There are only two possible meanings: mordents of some kind, or shakes with closing-notes. The latter can be dismissed; for there is no point in playing plain shakes in the first half of the Gigue, and shakes with closing-notes (∿✦) in the second half. There can be only one reason for changing the ornamentation in the second half: the shakes

of the first half are to be replaced by full-length mordents
(inverted shakes) in the second half, thus carrying the
inversion of the thematic material down to the details of the
ornamentation.

Ex. 289 will illustrate this point; and cf. Ex. 72.

Ex. 289   English Suite in D minor, Gigue.   Peters Urtext edition
bars 6–7   bars 30–31

Kreutz naturally recommends that the shakes in bar 6, etc.,
should begin on the main note, to make the inversion as
strict as possible.

As for the Schneller, Kreutz quotes Ex. 290.

Ex. 290   Two-part Invention in C minor, bar 13.   Autograph of 1723

It may be said that this ornament is unplayable, and must
therefore be a scribal error; but the following quotations from
the same piece cannot be set aside in this way (Ex. 291). All
four of these ornaments are in the autograph of 1723; those

Ex. 291
bar 3   bar 23   bar 25

in bars 3 and 23 are autograph in the Clavierbüchlein of
c. 1720 as well. According to the terminology used in this
book, they must be either Trillos or Schnellers; and as Trillos
would make consecutives, it follows that they must be
Schnellers.

The demonstration could hardly be more convincing.
J. S. Bach was using Schnellers in 1723 and earlier; and as
he used them in this Invention, one of his regular teaching
pieces, they must have been familiar to his pupils. This
accounts both for the tone of Emanuel Bach's description in
1753, and for the confusion that reigned between 1753 and
1789—points that I have discussed in Appendix I, and from
which I have argued laboriously backwards to the same
conclusion that Kreutz has reached by an entirely different
and more direct process.

It remains true that the Schneller is used too frequently,
considering that the sign ∿ has other meanings in Bach's
music. But there is no longer any question of its being
anachronistic; for Bach's employment of it has been proved
as conclusively as musicology can prove anything.

REPRODUCTIONS

THE reproductions overleaf will serve to illustrate certain ambiguities referred to in this book.

1. WK II, Prelude in E minor, bar 102. Autograph.
   Mordent and Turn.

2. Partita III, Allemande, bar 6. Original edition, 1731.
   The meaning of the first sign is uncertain: cf. p. 108.
   The second sign is a Short Shake.

3. Italian Concerto, first movement, bar 42. First Impression of the original edition, with manuscript corrections by Bach.
   Short Shake engraved as a straight line; *tww* superimposed in Bach's hand.

4. Same as no. 3, but from the Second Impression of the edition.
   Straight line replaced by an engraved ⋆⋆.

5. Italian Concerto, first movement, bars 110–12. First Impression of the original edition, with manuscript corrections by Bach.
   Long Shake engraved as a straight line; *tww* superimposed in Bach's hand.

6. Same as no. 5, but from the Second Impression of the edition.
   Straight line replaced by an engraved sign, apparently *cw*.

7. WK II, Fugue in C, bar 8. Autograph.
   Shake sign written across a stem.

8. WK II, Prelude in F sharp, bars 26–7. Autograph.
   Shakes (presumably long) with written-out closing-notes.

9. WK II, Prelude in E minor, bar 43. Autograph.
   Shake with appoggiatura opening.

10. WK II, Prelude in A minor, bar 16. Autograph.
    Shake with ascending prefix, and a final hook that may mean closing-notes.

11. WK II, Prelude in E minor, bars 77–8. Autograph.
    Shake with ascending prefix, final hook, and
    written-out closing-notes: also a Turn.
12. WK II, Prelude in B, bars 23–4. Autograph.
    Slide, and Nachschlags (or appoggiaturas) indicated
    by small notes.
13. WK II, Prelude in G sharp minor, bar 4. Autograph.
    Appoggiaturas indicated by single and double hooks.
14. Cantata 130, Oboe I, bar 21. Reputed autograph.
    Distorted *tr*.
15. Goldberg Variations, Aria, bars 1–2. Original edition,
    1742.
    Slurred Mordent (or Long Mordent), and appog-
    giaturas (or Nachschlags) indicated by small notes.
16. The same, bars 7–8.
    Appoggiatura moving by skip, and appoggiatura
    plus mordent.
17. The same, bars 11–12.
    Arpeggio, ᴄⱳ, Appoggiatura or Nachschlag, and
    ⱳ . The last sign in the example is not an orna-
    ment, but a 'direct' (like the catchwords in old
    books) showing the first note of the next line.

TABLE OF SIGNS

REFERENCES AND ABBREVIATIONS

AGRICOLA

Annotations to P. F. Tosi's *Introduction to the Art of Singing*, translated into German by J. F. Agricola (1720–74) under the title of *Anleitung zur Singkunst* (1757). Agricola was a pupil of J. S. Bach's about 1740.

ALDRICH

Putnam Aldrich, *Ornamentation in J. S. Bach's Organ Works*, New York, 1950.

BACH, C. P. EMANUEL

Versuch über die wahre Art das Clavier zu spielen. Part I, containing the section on ornaments, was first published in 1753. All quotations are taken from the revised edition of 1787. See also *Mitchell*.

References are given by section and paragraph, so that they apply both to the original and to Mitchell's translation. The following list gives the German equivalents of Mitchell's section-headings:

Embellishments, General	Von den Manieren überhaupt
The Appoggiatura	Von den Vorschlägen
The Trill	Von den Trillern
The Turn	Von dem Doppelschlage
The Mordent	Von dem Mordenten
The Slide	Von den Schleifern
The Snap (Schneller)	Von dem Schneller
Performance	Vom Vortrage

BACH, J. C. F.

The table of ornaments in *Musikalische Nebenstunden*, 1787.

BG

The Bach-Gesellschaft edition.

BISCHOFF

Hans Bischoff's edition of Bach's Clavier Works: Steingräber, Leipzig.

BWV

The numbers in W. Schmieder's Thematic Index (*Thematisch-systematisches Verzeichnis der musikalischen Werke von Johann Sebastian Bach*). Breitkopf, 1950.

COUPERIN (1713)

F. Couperin, *Pièces de Clavecin, Premier Livre.*

COUPERIN (1717)

F. Couperin, *L'Art de toucher le Clavecin.*

C.P.E.B.

Emanuel Bach.

D'ANGLEBERT

J. H. d'Anglebert, *Pièces de Clavecin*, 1689.

DANNREUTHER

Edward Dannreuther, *Musical Ornamentation.* Novello (out of print). A German version of his chapter on Bach is in Bach-Jahrbuch 1909, p. 41.

DAVID

H. T. David's edition of *Ouvertüre nach Französischer Art von J. S. Bach, ursprüngliche Fassung in c-moll.* Edition Schott no. 2380.

DOLMETSCH

Arnold Dolmetsch, *The Interpretation of the music of the seventeenth and eighteenth centuries.* Novello and Oxford University Press.

LANDSHOFF

Ludwig Landshoff's edition of Bach's *Inventions*, with *Revisionsbericht.* Peters Urtext series.

MARPURG (1749)

F. W. Marpurg, *Des critischen Musicus an der Spree, erster Band*: pp. 48, 54, 65, 79, 83. The collected edition of this periodical was published in 1750, but the relevant portions of it appeared in 1749.

MARPURG (1755, 1756)

F. W. Marpurg, *Anleitung zum Clavierspielen* (1755) and the French version *Principes du Clavecin* (1756).

MITCHELL
W. J. Mitchell's English translation of Emanuel Bach's *Versuch*, under the title *Essay on the true art of playing Keyboard Instruments.* Cassell, 1949; revised edition, 1951.

QUANTZ
J. J. Quantz, *Versuch einer Anweisung die Flöte traversiere zu spielen,* 1752.

TÜRK
D. G. Türk, *Klavierschule,* 1789.

WK I, II
The first and second parts of the Well-tempered Clavier.

XVIII
The so-called Eighteen Chorale Preludes: BG XXV. 2, Novello XVII, scattered alphabetically in Peters VI–VII.

Pitch Signs

LIST OF REFERENCES TO
BACH'S WORKS

THE references are to music examples unless the contrary
is stated.

Clavier

INDEX